SILENT

PEOPLE WITH MENTAL DISORDERS ON THE STREET

VOICES

ROBERT L. OKIN, MD

GOLDEN
PINE
PRESS

Mill Valley, California

For more information, contact:

GOLDEN
PINE
PRESS

38 Miller Avenue, #121
Mill Valley, CA 94941

Ordering Information:
Quantity sales. Special discounts are available on quantity purchases by corporations,
associations, and others. For details, contact the "Special Sales Department"
at the address above.

Orders by U.S. trade bookstores and wholesalers.
Please contact BCH: (800) 431-1579 or visit www.bookch.com for details.

All photos are courtesy of the author.

Book production consulting by Books by Brookes | www.booksbybrookes.com
Book and cover design by theBookDesigners | www.thebookdesigners.com

Publisher's Cataloging-in-Publication data

Okin, Robert L.
    Silent voices : people with mental disorders on the street / Robert L. Okin, M.D.
    p. cm.
    ISBN 978-0-9960777-0-5
1. Homeless persons --United States --Pictorial works. 2. Mentally ill homeless persons.
3. Homelessness --United States. 4. Homeless persons --United States --Portraits. I.
Title.

HV4505 .O35 2014
305.569 --dc23   2014937459

Printed in the United States of America on acid-free paper.

DEDICATION

This book is dedicated to the generous people on the street who believed their voices and images could make a difference in the world. Without their willingness to speak out and share themselves with me, this book would not have been possible.

And to the brave families of some of these people who have fought a never-ending battle for the people they love, in both the personal and political spheres.

AUTHOR'S NOTE

I approached most of the people I interviewed for this book more or less randomly, and without a prior introduction. Some were referred to me by their social workers. To ensure informed consent, I explained to each person that I wished to photograph him or her and obtain a first-person narrative about his or her life for inclusion in a book I was writing. I asked whether the person would be interested in participating in the project. I requested consent both before and after conducting each interview or taking photographs. Thus, the person had an opportunity to withdraw his or her consent after hearing and answering my questions or having photographs taken. Only those individuals who consented both before *and* after the interview and the photography are included here. The individuals whose photographs appear on pages 57–59, 128, and 167 gave their consent to be photographed for the book but were not interviewed. Thus, although I encountered them on the street, I do not know for certain whether they were homeless or mentally ill.

CONTENTS

INTRODUCTION

I was sitting on a bench near the Ferry Building in San Francisco, waiting for a friend and watching the sun come up over the bay, when a middle-aged black man sat down next to me. I had seen him a few minutes earlier pushing a shopping cart loaded with his clothes, sleeping bag, and other possessions. Despite the 85-degree heat, he was covered in several layers of thick woolen clothing and was completely hooded. Only his eyes were visible. As I turned to him, he began whispering silently to himself and then to the bell that clanged in the tower of the Ferry Building at 15-minute intervals. "Who are you talking to?" I asked him. "God," he responded. "How do you get in touch with him?" I pursued. "Through the bell," he whispered and abruptly stood up and walked away, pushing his cart in front of him.

A few minutes later, I watched a woman dressed in rags, with nothing on her feet, pulling a train of three carts loaded with what seemed like odds and ends. She stopped suddenly in the middle of the street, gesticulated wildly to the passing traffic, and went on her way.

In the next half hour, I saw a blue sleeping bag floating down the sidewalk. The young woman inside of it dug into each trash can along her path. Occasionally, she'd find a half-finished, discarded cup of coffee and would drink what was left of it. I walked up to her and offered to take her to a coffee shop around the corner. She came with me and told me she'd come to San Francisco from Italy for a vacation but couldn't remember from which city or when. After nibbling on a bun, like a little mouse, she excused herself politely and walked out. I saw her several

times after that, walking around the area, dragging her sleeping bag behind her, never talking to anyone. On one occasion, she disrobed in the middle of the public square, replacing her sweatshirt with a lighter garment.

I found myself totally absorbed by these people as they made their way silently around the city. I had been interested in people with severe mental illness throughout my professional career, from the time I was commissioner of mental health for the states of Vermont and Massachusetts through my 17 years as chief of psychiatry at San Francisco General Hospital and professor of clinical psychiatry at UCSF. In each of these positions, I designed programs for severely mentally ill people so they could live with dignity in the community. While most people, with this support, could be treated outside the walls of hospitals, budgetary constraints prevented us from developing the programs necessary to reach all the people who needed help.

Even with my considerable experience, I was always bewildered by how the mentally ill living on the street managed to survive when programs were unavailable to them. When I retired from my position at the hospital, I decided to find out. I wanted to get closer to these people in order to hear from them about their lives directly and personally. I wanted to understand how they coped with their illnesses and the stresses of homelessness and jail. I wanted to know what they thought about as they pushed their carts down the street, what they did with their empty time, how they managed at night, and why they made some of the choices they did. I wanted to know how they dealt with being "moved along" or arrested by the police when they were discovered sleeping on park benches. I wanted to know how they dealt with being so utterly shunned by society.

I wanted to know how they showered, where they relieved themselves when there were no public toilets at hand, and how some developed the motivation to get off drugs when life on the street was so stressful, barren, and discouraging, and when there was nothing else to look forward to but the next fix. I wanted to understand why they so often refused to take their psychiatric medications, why some preferred to live outside in the cold and rain than in shelters or transient hotels, and why in the world any of them would choose to live in foggy San Francisco rather than balmy San Diego or Los Angeles. In a sense, I wanted to see these people beyond their rags, their carts, their tin cups, and their strange behaviors. I wanted to see the ways they were the same as I was, not just the ways they were different.

To answer these questions, I decided I had to leave my office in the hospital and meet these people where they lived. I had to ask them if they would speak to me about their lives—their joys, sorrows, struggles, and triumphs. I had to try to see what it was like to live in their skin and walk in their shoes, enveloped in so much isolation and silence. I decided to spend time with them on the street, in their rooms, in court, and in shelters. This was the only way I was going to get the kind of nitty-gritty knowledge I was seeking. It was the only way I was going to understand what life was like from their point of view.

MY APPROACH TO THIS PROJECT

My original plan was simply to start up conversations with people I met on the street, hope they wouldn't think I was too weird, and ask them if they would talk to me about their lives. But after a few encounters, I was so intrigued and moved by some of their stories that I developed a wish to share them with a larger audience. I wanted to convey the human face of mental disorders as a counterweight to the fear, hostility, and indifference with which mentally ill people are generally seen and portrayed. By giving them a voice in the public domain, I wanted to enable them to convey their longings, regrets, joys, anxieties, hopes—their essential humanity.

My initial intention was to focus on people who were presumptively diagnosable with mental disorders, at least from my observations on the street. But in time, it became clear to me, as it had in clinical contexts, that a very large number of people I met didn't fit neatly into formal diagnostic categories. Nevertheless, many of them were extremely troubled; were doing poorly in their lives by any standard; and were suffering from some combination of genetic vulnerability, difficult family situations, childhood abuse, traumas of war, drug addiction, poverty, and social marginalization. Most seemed to be missing certain crucial capacities needed to function normally in society. It was people within this broader definition of what it means to be mentally ill that I decided to include in this book. Some of the individuals I chose to interview were involved in mental health programs and were referred to me by their social workers. The vast majority, however, I approached directly and spontaneously on the street without any introduction.

I always talked to people privately, though often in relatively public places—standing or sitting on a street corner or in a coffee shop, subway station, or park. Early in my interactions with these individuals, I was struck by the beauty and expressiveness of their faces as they deeply and authentically told me about their lives. So I began asking people if I could take their photographs while we were talking. I decided not to pose them in front of a black or white background even though this might have led to greater artistic effect, because I didn't want to decontextualize them from the physical circumstances of their lives. When choices had to be made, I strove for authenticity over drama.

MY EXPERIENCE ON THE STREET

When I first went onto the street, I wasn't certain I would be able to engage people to participate, especially when I explained that I wished to record their narratives and take their photographs while they spoke to me. I discovered, however, that most of the people I met agreed to participate, frequently after I was able to overcome their initial mistrust, anxiety, shame, and anger. Many were willing to talk to me with surprising candor and feeling about very intimate issues. They often spoke with tears in their eyes.

AN ETHICAL DILEMMA

Especially at times of intense emotion, I was concerned about how probing to be, even though these people had given me explicit consent to record and photograph them. Had this consent really been informed? I sometimes asked myself. Had they really known what they were getting into? Did they really want their voices to be heard when they were conveying stories that were so intimate and potentially so embarrassing? Regarding informed consent, I was careful to ask for consent both before and after conducting an interview or taking photographs. Thus, the person had an opportunity to withdraw his or her consent after hearing and answering my questions or having photographs taken. Only those individuals who consented both before *and* after the interview or the photography are included

here. (I describe my consent methodology in greater detail in the Author's Note at the beginning of the book.) Beyond the issue of formal consent, it seemed disrespectful, unfeeling, intrusive, and incredibly awkward to raise the camera between us and click the shutter at these vulnerable moments, recording forever the images of their distress. Yet my wish to convey to readers the depth of feeling so many mentally ill people were silently bearing, buried under their more visible symptoms, was one of the main reasons for the project. It was this very depth of feeling that I hoped readers might relate to.

Although my intent was fundamentally altruistic, I was often haunted by a concern that I was spying into the misery of other people's lives partially out of my own voyeuristic interest. I was often worried that I was using, exposing, and exploiting people whom life had already treated so poorly. I was a total stranger, yet I was asking people to expose their personal lives to me and to the public, even when this might be painful and, in some cases, humiliating. It is hardly surprising that, at times, I felt I had no right to be on the street and that the enterprise was somehow illegitimate, even though I had diligently obtained the consent of the people I was writing about.

WHY THEY PARTICIPATED

I began to feel more comfortable in my interviews as I recognized that most of the people who agreed to participate felt that they were receiving something in return—the possibility of being seen and heard, by me and perhaps by others, and of having some kind of impact in the world. Many participants had never been listened to as children, felt voiceless and invisible as adults, and were certain that no one would notice or miss them when they were gone. Having their words and images recorded seemed to give them tangible evidence that the universe had taken note of their existence, that they would leave their footprints in the sand. For some people, participating fulfilled a deep wish to do something they regarded as socially useful—to warn, to teach, to inspire, and to demonstrate that it was possible to do something constructive in the world. They shared their experiences to counter both their own and society's perception of them as useless—or worse, destructive.

Those individuals who had been referred to me by mental health programs universally expressed the hope that by participating, they could give back to staff members who had truly cared about them—and even, in some cases, saved their lives. For these people, participation was an act of public gratitude, an opportunity to pay tribute to the staff's work in a very personal way.

GOOD DAYS AND BAD DAYS

In the early days of the project, I was very anxious. One reason was that I felt like the ultimate outsider, the well-heeled, camera-toting guy who clearly didn't belong on the street. Being on the street gave me a small taste of what it was like to be "the other." The sense of being different, of not fitting in, was extremely disturbing on some primal level, despite the fact that some of the ways I was different obviously gave me certain advantages in life. Moreover, I was the supplicant, the one who needed help and cooperation rather than the person who could give these things. I was the one asking for a handout—in the form of photographs and stories. I was the panhandler with the tin cup who could be ignored, derided, or dismissed. This was the worst part of the whole experience for me.

Although people were generally very friendly to me, there were some painful exceptions. Sometimes they regarded me with a degree of mistrust that I was unable to break through, and they dismissed me with a wave of the hand. This was particularly the case when a lot of methamphetamine was available on the street. More people than usual were high, irritable, suspicious, volatile, and very crazy. At these times, I was afraid that even looking at someone too directly might be experienced as provocative and lead to an angry eruption. Perhaps because I was careful, this never happened to me in any serious way, though I had a couple of trivial encounters. On one occasion, a young man saw me photographing someone, believed I hadn't asked permission, and concluded I was being disrespectful. He hurled an apple at me, catching me in the chest. He later apologized when I confronted him about it. In another instance, a woman became suddenly and unexpectedly angry about my approaching her, picked up her crutch, and threatened me with it.

I met several people who were difficult to understand because their thoughts were so scrambled and delusional. These people might have been easily dismissed as "crazy" because they seemed to be living in internal worlds that were intensely dangerous and infuriating. Frequently, the people who appeared to be the most enraged and explosive were also the most scared. Some of them may, in fact, have been hurt or invaded earlier in their lives, and were expressing their enduring reactions to these experiences in the only language they knew. Being with these people was always an unsettling experience, the more so when I was finally able to pick disturbing themes out of their confusing thoughts.

I often felt exhausted and drained at the end of the day and couldn't imagine how I was going to get back onto the street again the next morning. Wandering around in the absence of a clear-cut agenda often felt aimless and unfocused. I often wondered how the people I met could tolerate this kind of life as their steady diet. Occasionally, after spending time with people who were very disorganized and psychotic, I felt disoriented and off-balance myself. Even when people spoke to me in a way I understood, I frequently found what they said disturbing. Their stories of bleakness and misfortune often left me with a lump in my throat and an overwhelming sense of loneliness, isolation, and despair. At these times, I couldn't seem to separate my life from theirs, and felt only an inch away from falling off the same edge that had crumbled beneath their feet.

Lest I convey the impression that my experience on the street was mostly anxious or sad, I need to emphasize how many "good days" I had. Most people I talked to were welcoming, interesting, and smart; made me feel comfortable; and conveyed their belief that I was engaged in something valuable. Some people were funny and entertaining, seemed to genuinely enjoy their lives, and showed me a different side to my own. Equally pleasurable was being challenged by new experiences and forced to question certain cherished assumptions. Best of all, and a bonus that has lasted long after the conclusion of the project, were enduring friendships with several of the people I met.

PERSONAL INVOLVEMENT

Almost as soon as I began meeting people, I struggled with the question of how involved to become in their lives. Taking a detached and "objective" position, assuming a more classically anthropological approach, limiting myself to observing, recording, bearing witness, and in a sense remaining on the outside of their experience, seemed to undermine my original intention of understanding their lives more deeply. My decision was ultimately influenced less by these intellectual considerations than by my inability to resist the pull to become involved with certain people who welcomed me into their lives. In some cases, it seemed simply like the right thing to do. In other cases, I became quite attached to them and felt nourished by the give and take, informality, mutual acceptance, and ease of the relationship.

I tried to help some of these people with the issues they were struggling with, sometimes to good effect and sometimes to no effect. There are few experiences so illuminating, and so humbling, as trying to help someone solve an apparently simple practical problem, and failing miserably. Notwithstanding these failures when they occurred, I was always surprised at how simple acts of human kindness could make such a seemingly large difference. Although I may have sacrificed a certain amount of objectivity by my real-life involvement, I believe that I gained a much deeper understanding of people's lives than would have been possible with a more detached approach.

FROM JUDGMENT TO ADMIRATION

Contributing to my initial anxiety were my negative judgments of the people I was talking to—the very judgments I was struggling

against. The result was that I initially couldn't figure out how to explain the project to the people I approached in a way they were likely to view as respectful and supportive, rather than shaming and denigrating. However artfully I put my request, I feared they would detect my underlying critique, as though I was saying, "Excuse me, sir, I'm interested in talking with you because you look so colorfully beaten up by life, like you can't cope." Or, "Excuse me, ma'am, you look like a real screw-up who's made a total mess of your life. It would really be fascinating to hear about how you accomplished this. Moreover, with your permission, I'd love to spread the story of your unhappy life, along with your picture, all over the public domain. Would that be okay?" Was it any wonder I expected people to turn me down?

As I got to know certain people, the negative stereotypes I was secretly harboring (and the fears I had of people's negative stereotypes of me) gradually melted away. Making contact with these individuals and hearing their stories helped me genuinely appreciate what most of them had been up against from the day they were born, and what they were still dealing with day after day. Even when I saw how they were actively contributing to their unhappy lives, something that used to infuriate me, I began to understand why they were doing it. I could see that their "bad" choices were driven by forces that felt irresistible to them. With experience and exposure, my original judgments were replaced by admiration, and by the nagging and uncomfortable question of how I would have fared with the miserable hand that life had dealt them.

A BRIEF HISTORY OF THE HOMELESS MENTALLY ILL

To understand the situation of the homeless mentally ill today, it is helpful to look at the past. Homelessness of the mentally ill in the United States is the combined effect of the prejudices of the culture and the policies of multiple governmental systems. It has resulted from successive, incomplete reforms that moved the mentally ill from poorhouses in the eighteenth century to state hospitals in the nineteenth century to shelters, prisons, and the street in the latter half of the twentieth century. (For a more detailed account, please see Appendix B, "History of the Homeless Mentally Ill.")

During the eighteenth and early nineteenth centuries, people with mental disorders who could not be cared for otherwise often ended up in almshouses or jails. In these settings, they were frequently mistreated. In the second quarter of the nineteenth century, state legislatures, lobbied by social activists, created asylums to protect and treat people with mental disorders. Many patients, after relatively short stays, were able to return to their families and communities considerably improved. While primarily driven by humanitarian impulses, these facilities also served the darker purpose of isolating and segregating the mentally ill from the rest of society.

After the Civil War, state hospitals found themselves flooded with more patients than they could handle. The previously small, well-staffed, relatively humane asylums became large, understaffed institutions. Inmates had no civil rights, received little treatment, and were disconnected from their families and communities. Under these adverse conditions, many patients who formerly would have been treated successfully and discharged became "incurable" lifelong residents. By the early 1900s, these institutions became dumping grounds for social rejects, including the mentally ill. Once patients were locked inside, it was often very difficult to get out.

In the mid-1950s, it was discovered that the anesthetic chlorpromazine (Thorazine) could ameliorate the psychotic symptoms of certain patients. The process of deinstitutionalization—the aggressive discharge and restricted admission of patients—began. State governments, civil rights attorneys, and mental health professionals all supported the policy. But when the fixed costs of state hospitals remained high and funds couldn't be redirected to create community services despite the reduced number of patients, state governments declined responsibility for the care of discharged patients. Many less functional patients found themselves isolated and struggling in their communities after their discharge from hospitals.

The 1970s drug epidemic in the United States prompted many patients to turn to street drugs for physical and emotional comfort. These drugs frequently aggravated their underlying psychiatric symptoms, further compromised their diminished sense of impulse control, and weakened their motivation for treatment. They increased patients' vulnerability to predators on the street, involved them in criminal activities, pushed them into the correctional system, and increased their risk of dying from drug-related complications. Drugs, mental disorders, homelessness, and incarceration became a vicious cycle from which many never escaped.

In the 1960s, the federal government for the first time began to accept some responsibility for the welfare of poor, untreated patients in the community. Congress enacted legislation to ameliorate some of the harshest conditions, but these efforts never went far enough. Adequate treatment, housing, jobs, and economic support largely remained unrealized ideals. Hundreds of thousands of untreated mentally ill people were forced by their poverty to live in dilapidated transient hotels with no personal bathrooms, showers, or kitchens. Worse, some drifted to the street, where they lived with nothing. The gentrification of low-income housing, two recessions, and the government's meager monetary support for the poor and disabled contributed to the movement of the mentally ill to the street.

To save people from the cruelest conditions of the street, many cities created temporary shelters. Unfortunately, these refuges were often poorly designed and insufficiently funded. They didn't have enough beds, and the close quarters put individuals at risk of contracting contagious diseases. Many shelters developed a reputation for being ill-supervised and dangerous. They often failed to provide locked personal storage space, making possessions vulnerable to theft. Over the years, thousands gave up on shelters and decided to take their chances sleeping on the street.

Meanwhile, the health care system was gaining an increasing share of society's resources. Private and public hospital reimbursement became available for psychiatric patients. Therefore, patients could be treated in their local communities, and inpatient psychiatric care was brought into the mainstream of modern medicine. Over time, however, state and federal governments and private insurance companies became less and less willing to pay for psychiatric inpatient treatment in general hospitals; as a result, these hospitals shortened the length of stays for even the most disturbed patients. Patients were admitted and discharged so rapidly that it was impossible for many to be stabilized before being sent back to their homes, shelters, or the street.

Another phenomenon that contributed to the growing number of untreated patients in the community was the enactment of more rigorous commitment laws. These made it more difficult to commit patients to hospitals and restricted the time they could be confined there. Physicians had to substantiate that mentally ill people posed an imminent threat of serious physical harm to themselves or others, or were unable to meet their basic needs. Otherwise, they could not be hospitalized against their will, no matter how psychotic they were. This increased respect for people's civil rights prevented unnecessary hospitalizations, but often at the expense of their mental health. Were adequate alternatives available, it would have been possible to treat many of these people on a voluntary outpatient basis without either restricting their liberty through forced hospitalization or abandoning them because they failed to meet standards for commitment. The choice of involuntary hospitalization or no treatment at all, which prevailed during most of the state hospital era, is being repeated in the general hospital era.

In the end, many people were not spared a restriction of their liberty, even when they couldn't be hospitalized against their will. Because certain patients could no longer be committed to hospitals, police brought them to jail instead. Tighter commitment standards for hospitalization ironically led to increased confinement in jails and prisons. The number of mentally ill people in the criminal justice system today is estimated to be 250,000. It is generally agreed that the use of jails for most people who are mentally ill is ineffective as a deterrent, counterproductive as an economic policy, harmful as a clinical intervention, and offensive to the most elementary sense of justice. Nevertheless, this form of isolating and confining people with mental disorders continues to operate largely under the radar.

PATHS TO BECOMING MENTALLY ILL AND HOMELESS

This book presents the stories of people who are both mentally ill and homeless. Most people with mental illness do not become homeless, and vice versa. But mental illness can lead to homelessness when people's symptoms become so severe that their functioning is impaired. Their resulting poverty pushes them onto the street. Conversely, the stresses of homelessness increase the likelihood that someone on the margin of mental illness will be forced over the edge. It is the particular interaction between biological vulnerability, severe environmental experiences, and street drugs that can lead to both mental illness and homelessness.

Some people I interviewed probably came into the world genetically vulnerable to mental illness. Others were abused and neglected at an early age; began failing in school due to an inability to concentrate; turned to drugs in adolescence, which complicated their learning problems; and developed mental illness in late adolescence or early adulthood as a result of one or several of these factors. Failing to graduate from high school, whatever the cause, many entered adulthood without marketable skills and never made it into the job market. Without an early employment history, they had nothing to parlay into future job opportunities. Others, even if they managed to get through adolescence without obvious symptoms, suffered some trauma or serious reversal as adults (for example, warfare experiences or significant personal losses), turned to drugs to numb their intense emotional reactions to these events, and became more, not less, symptomatic.

CHILDHOOD TRAUMAS AND SEXUAL ABUSE

The vast majority of people I spoke to had experienced multiple traumas in childhood. Most had parents who were neglectful, drug-addicted, and abusive. Some parents were severely mentally ill. The individuals I interviewed relayed accounts of being regularly beaten, verbally assaulted, or abandoned as children; of living in constant fear for their safety; or of being drawn into the drug culture by older siblings or their own parents. The mother of one man was so violent that on separate occasions, she shot her husband and heaved him through a plate-glass window. The father of one man put his son's feet to a fire, severely burning him for misbehaving.

Almost half of the homeless mentally ill women I met had been sexually abused as children, sometimes violently. Whereas I had expected that many would have experienced sexual abuse, accompanied by maternal neglect, during childhood, I was unprepared for how prevalent this was. Many turned to drugs

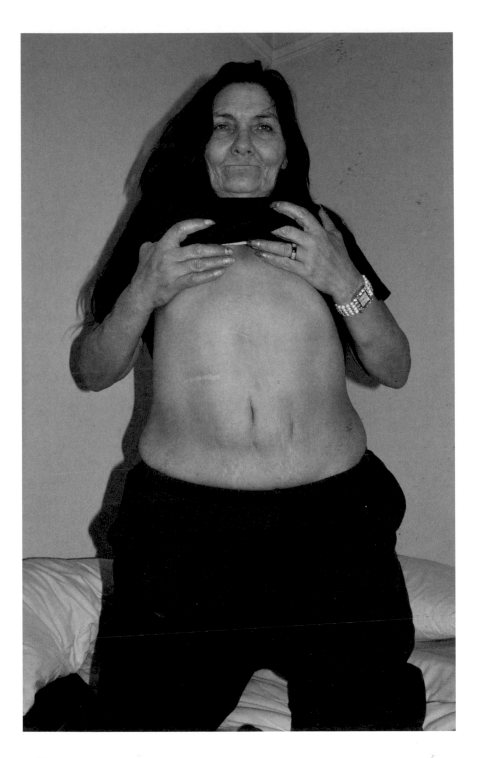

and promiscuous sex in adolescence to blunt the painful emotional consequences of these early experiences, but these choices set them up for further sexual and emotional abuse. Most became homeless through their use of drugs, economic catastrophe, psychiatric symptoms, or the belief that they deserved nothing better in life.

Whatever their genetic vulnerability, it was clear that childhood traumas and sexual abuse had also permanently wounded the people I talked to, truncated their emotional development, and led to pervasive functional deficits in adulthood. It is easy to forget the impact of such experiences when we pass these people on the street, especially when all we can see are the outward signs of their poverty and their odd conduct. In fact, it is easy to forget they were children at all.

DRUG ADDICTION

The lives of a large number of the people I met in the course of writing this book revolved around getting, using, and recovering from drugs. For most of these people, several factors converged to perpetuate their drug use, making drugs almost irresistible. These factors included a biological vulnerability to addiction; identification with parents who used; neglect and abuse in childhood; involvement in drug-using social networks in adolescence; extreme poverty in adulthood; and an inability to cope with painful feelings of depression, rage, boredom, psychotic symptoms, post-traumatic stress, and so on.

The majority of people who resorted to alcohol and drugs as a consistent part of their lives dug themselves into a pit of unemployability. Both the altered states of consciousness these substances brought about in the short term and the personality changes they caused in the long term sapped these individuals' mental and physical energy, and killed their drive and ambition. Drugs made it almost impossible for them to plan, organize, remember, get themselves to places on time, execute their intentions, and handle the interpersonal stress associated with even low-level jobs. The impairment of these functions was further compromised by other symptoms of mental disorder. Once they began living on the street, many became ensnared in a cycle of homelessness and joblessness.

Several individuals had spent time in jail or prison for possession and sale of drugs, and some for theft they engaged in to maintain their addictions. One man stole $200 worth of merchandise every day to support his habit. He was jailed three times and only escaped going to prison for a year through the intervention of his social worker. Some of the women used prostitution to pay for drugs. Almost everyone I spoke to had several friends who had died from drug overdoses or other complications of addiction.

Given the destructiveness of drugs, it is natural to wonder why people don't just stop using, as if getting off were simply an act of will. Some individuals seem to find the inner strength to quit, but often they have to reach a point of desperation first. Those people I spoke to who escaped from the drug life were able to do so only with the help of specialized treatment programs—and when they were looking death in the eye. Drugs are an almost inescapable way of numbing oneself to the hardships of life on the street, and giving them up by oneself is almost impossible. As one man put it, "Living on the street is so bad, you have to be either stoned or crazy to bear it."

PERSONAL LOSSES

I expected to encounter impenetrability, hardened shells, and resistance when I asked people on the street about their lives, but the majority seemed genuinely to welcome the chance to unburden themselves to another person. Most were coping with intense grief about very painful issues in their lives and had been unable to resolve the losses and traumas that had occurred often many years before. I was totally unprepared

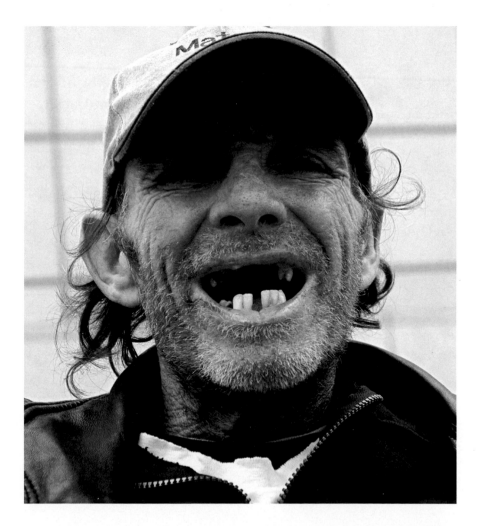

for how close to the surface these feelings were. No matter how "tough" these people first appeared, they became openly tearful at some point during our talks. They evinced sadness, regret, rage, depression, and guilt over personal calamities such as betrayal by a spouse, firing from a job, abandonment by a parent, or death of a spouse or child. These losses, along with the other issues they were coping with, led to a collapse in their ability to function and ultimately to their state of homelessness.

BARELY GETTING BY

Most of the people I spoke to were barely getting by, if that. Sometimes they were able to sustain themselves on the street through government subsidies, but often they survived through a variety of ingenious, if sometimes illegal, means. Some of them traded prescribed medications for street drugs. Others prostituted for money or drugs, shoplifted, panhandled, or hustled. Some took food out of dumpsters or ate in soup kitchens. Others sold bottles and cans to recycling centers for a little cash.

PUBLIC ASSISTANCE

People with certain forms of mental disorders are eligible for government support in the form of Supplemental Security Income (SSI). But applying for SSI is a long, complicated, and frustrating process involving a great deal of documentation and multiple denials, often taking months or years before applications are approved. Total and permanent disability is the government's standard for approving a person for SSI.

Some of the most disorganized people in this book were never able to navigate the process precisely because they were so disorganized. Others were deemed technically ineligible for one reason or another, sometimes because they could not get a doctor to advocate for them, at other times because they didn't have access to the requisite paperwork. Yet some were able to obtain some form of public assistance and housing; they had usually been vigorously assisted by social workers who were dedicated to helping them. These were the lucky ones. They illustrate what is possible with concrete human assistance.

REACTIONS TO LIVING ON THE STREET

Most of the people I met during the course of this project had lived on the street for years, enduring various situations, such as sleeping on a heating grate, being hosed down by the city's street cleaning trucks early in the morning, or living in a tent in the hills and being hunted down by police. Many described their difficulty finding public bathrooms and the humiliation of being forced to urinate or defecate between buildings or in the bushes. As one man, who was able to get a room with the help of his social worker, told me, "I'd kill myself if I had to go back to the streets. Once you've been inside, there is no way you can go back out there again."

While most found sleeping on the street intolerable, several told me that they actually preferred it to the housing options available to them. A number of individuals said they lived outside because even the most miserable hotel room cost over $600 a month. Those who were not receiving government support couldn't afford even this. Many others who did receive support ($850/month) did not want to spend it on housing, since this would have left them with almost nothing to pay for any other expenses in their lives. One man preferred to use his SSI money for headphones, watches, and so on; other people preferred to use this money for drugs. Additional reasons people gave for choosing to live outside included the distraction from their inner demons provided by dealing with the constant physical demands of survival, freedom from the social pressures of living with others, a dislike of confinement, a fear of catching others' infections, a fear of being preyed upon by other clients, and simply an attraction to the freedom of the street. Still others were so suspicious and paranoid about others that sleeping close to them stirred up their anxiety and psychotic fears and caused them to choose the street over shelters.

OBSTACLES TO GETTING AND KEEPING A JOB

Living outside creates serious obstacles to getting and keeping a job, making it difficult to escape from the homeless condition. Homelessness makes it tough to get or stay clean for a job interview because people are constantly out in the elements, getting rained and blown on, and absorbing the exhaust, grime, and dirt of the street. Many men told me with embarrassment that although they were afraid their bodies and clothes smelled, they found it almost impossible to clean up because they didn't have easy access to showers and had no clean clothes.

Even if they could get hold of some presentable clothes, they had no place to store them. No matter how diligent they were about their possessions, they frequently lost them or had them stolen. Anything they didn't actually have their hands around, and many things they did, had a habit of "walking away." And even if they did manage to snag a job, they had no place to keep their possessions while they were working. They couldn't very well push their shopping cart through the front door of the business that just hired them and ask the person at the front desk to guard it while they worked.

Further, homeless people lack contact information to give to prospective employers. Without an address or telephone number, a homeless person has no obvious way for a prospective employer to contact him or her, so the employer will simply call the next person on the list, someone who is reachable. Even if a homeless person secures an interview, an admission of homelessness often prompts the next question—about his or her drug and alcohol history, and after that, his or her criminal history. The shame of opening up about all of this and then being rejected for it is too much for most of these people, especially because they suspect that even if they could get in the front door and actually get the job, they wouldn't be able to do it.

This is not evidence of some neurotic, unrealistic lack of confidence. It reflects a view of themselves that has been well-earned by repeated experience. Because so many of the people in this situation see themselves as failures, they have little trust that they can do anything other than panhandle, hustle, or depend on the government. Even if their external manner is aggressive, demanding, or entitled, this is usually a defensive façade. Most are convinced that they have no right to expect anything from anyone, because they see themselves as such total losers.

It could be argued that not all of these obstacles to regular employment are insurmountable. There are places, though not very accessible, that homeless people can bathe. They could wash themselves in a public bathroom, although this is easier said than done. They could scrape together enough cash to get a clean pair of pants, a shirt, and some decent shoes. And they could get a friend to watch their cart and possessions while they interviewed for a job.

Some of us, no doubt, could pull ourselves out of this cycle— especially if we were smart, had stable and non-abusive early life histories, had someone in our childhoods who loved and believed in us, and particularly if we did okay in school. Some of us could learn the survival skills needed to function in a complicated, highly technical society, especially if we had no addictions, no serious medical or psychiatric problems, and some source of social support. But without these advantages, it is doubtful that most of us would be able to find and keep a job. It is usually the combination and interaction of personal limitations and circumstantial obstacles that defeat people in the end, even if one or the other alone could be surmounted. And luck has a lot to do with this.

PANHANDLING

Even for street-savvy guys, panhandling is tough, unreliable, boring, and poorly paid, requiring a huge amount of patience, tenacity, and a tough outer shell. What people who panhandle hate most about it is the indifference, annoyance, and contempt with which they are regarded. I once spent a morning with someone who panhandled, and I calculated that in the course of a six-hour day, rain or shine, he was passed by 25,000 cars and averaged .06 cent per car, which translated to $2.50 an hour. Whatever one thinks about the ethics of panhandling, it is an inefficient way to make a living. Moreover, anyone who thinks panhandling is easy and people who do it are simply lazy should try it for a few hours in the winter, or even the summer, and see whether they still think so.

So why do people panhandle? Not because they're lazy. Basically, they do it because they're poor and out of other options. They're functionally unemployable, either because they are caught in the cycle of homelessness and joblessness, or because of their drug use, lack of motivation, psychiatric symptoms, or functional deficits. And although not technically disabled by federal or state standards, many people who panhandle have either been deemed ineligible for public assistance or can't navigate the application process.

AGAINST ALL ODDS

In the course of this project, there were individuals who, against all odds, extracted themselves from life on the street, drug addiction, crime, and prostitution. Several of the people I met were real success stories. With the right combination of services, they were able to shake their addictions, take their psychiatric medications, get into supportive housing, and transform their lives. One man, who had suffered for 10 years with severe addiction and depression, is now drug-free, living in an apartment, and working part-time. Another man, after fighting severe depression and alcoholism, living on the street, and eating from garbage cans, was ultimately coaxed into a support system, where he is now working as an assistant manager of a homeless kitchen. One woman, after living as a drug-addicted prostitute on the street, was able to make use of a case manager, a drug program, and housing to free herself from drugs and the lifestyle required to support her habit. Another woman, who struggled with bipolar disorder and alternately lived in shelters and on a bus, was finally helped by a case manager to find a subsidized apartment and take psychiatric medications.

Breaking the Cycle
of Social Stigma

The negative views I held of people with mental disorders going into this journey were only slowly dislodged by my experiences. It is disheartening to recognize that these views are so tenacious. Sociological studies show that even when we intellectually know better, we respond to these disorders with fear, anger, scorn, blame, and disparagement. We continue to view homelessness and mental disorders as evidence of some deep personal flaw, proof of some intrinsic badness or guilt, a sign that the person suffering from them has done, thought, or felt something terribly wrong and therefore carries a permanent stain on his or her fundamental humanity.

Not only are these reactions ubiquitous, they are often as destructive as the disorders themselves. They not only wreak havoc with people's self-regard, evoking shame, guilt, self-hatred, and despair, but they also have very tangible and destructive social, economic, and political consequences that intimately affect people's lives. Almost everyone I spoke to carried the scars of this stigma.

The people I met had internalized these attitudes. Their predominant characterization of themselves was, "I'm a fuck-up!" Even though some recognized that the deck had been stacked against them from early in their lives, this in no way made them less self-forgiving. What they dwelt on most were the ways they had sabotaged themselves, disappointed others, and rejected offers of help. As one man put it so eloquently, "If you have a big nose, well, no one can blame you. It's just the way you were born. But if you have no teeth, it's proof that you've fucked up real bad and that you must be nothing but a fuck-up."

While at first blush there may be some evidence to support this kind of self-condemnation, even the most cursory look at the lives of these people reveals that this is only part of the story. For the vast majority of people who were willing to talk with me, the trajectory of self-sabotage was set early in life by their biological vulnerabilities and their wounding childhoods. Their own contribution to messing up their lives, though real, was more an effect for which they deserved understanding than a cause for which they deserved blame.

Beyond the immediate impact of stigma on the individual's self-worth, optimism, sense of efficacy, and motivation, the negative branding associated with mental disorders also has powerful effects at social, economic, and political levels. Reducing people to some "flaw," viewing them as fundamentally different, negates our ability to identify and empathize with them, and leads to a perception that they are somehow less human than the rest of us. When a group of people is viewed as less human, others with more social capital feel entitled to treat them as such. Examples include Jews following the establishment of Christianity, women branded as witches in colonial North America, enslaved African Americans in the United States, etc. This entitlement to dehumanize, enforced by social power, has almost no limits. The devalued group, particularly if also feared and blamed, as in the case of people with mental disorders, finds itself subject to the most extreme forms of neglect and abuse. People with mental disorders have almost never escaped this fate. Throughout history, millions have been beaten, chained, banished to the countryside, or reduced to living in barns and pigsties. But this is not simply their *history*: this treatment is occurring today, with 200,000 abandoned in the street, and another 250,000 incarcerated in jails and prisons. This is, of course, an understatement of the problem, because an even larger number of mentally ill people are subject to other forms of legally sanctioned discrimination and neglect in almost all spheres of life, most notably in health care, housing, and jobs. The consequences of this can be found in their untreated symptoms and abject poverty.

Ironically, many of the characteristics that make these people seem strange and different from us are not an intrinsic part of their disorders but a result of our social and political decision to keep them impoverished. The features of their poverty (toothlessness, tattered clothes, shopping carts, and other aspects of their lives on the street) in turn make them look stranger and weirder than they would otherwise, which intensifies our reluctance to share our resources with them. And the cycle reinforces itself.

And then there is the pervasive sense of hopelessness we have about these people, a belief that there is no intervention that would "get them off the street." This contributes to our tendency to "vote against them" at the ballot box, to deny them the resources they need. It is common to hear legislators justifying their reluctance to spend money on services for the mentally ill by arguing that allocating funds for this purpose would be like "throwing money down a rathole"; that is, it would have no real effect. My conclusion from the work I've done in the hospital and on the street has always confirmed my conviction that most people, no matter how dramatic their presentation, can be helped, and that the gap between what we know can help these people and what we are actually doing as a society to help is enormous. The hopelessness with which we approach this problem has become a self-fulfilling prophecy.

Perhaps this cycle would be less tenacious if it were not reinforced by another that involves our tendency to avoid any meaningful contact with these people. Our avoidance, the ways we remain deaf to their stories and blind to their faces, has the effect of nailing in and reinforcing our conviction that they are fundamentally different from us, because we never really give ourselves the chance to develop another perspective. We don't see that beneath their symptoms and rags are people struggling in their own ways with intense feelings and needs, most of which are similar to our own. And this, in turn, contributes to our tendency to shun them, because they continue to seem so foreign, different, and strange. One of the reasons I wrote this book was to contribute to making these people known as human beings, thus reducing this pernicious cycle of social stigma. Perhaps the reader, on seeing their faces and listening to their stories, will come to regard them with a new perspective. Perhaps he or she will then vote differently at the ballot box when services for mentally ill homeless people are on the budgetary chopping block. Perhaps then these people will finally have a chance in life.

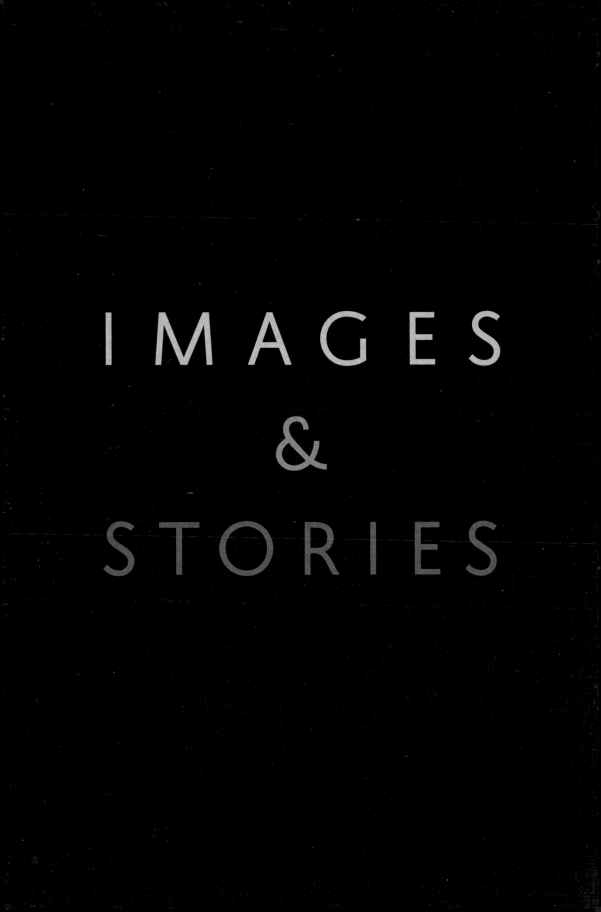

IMAGES
&
STORIES

No person shall sit, lie or sleep in or upon any street, sidewalk or other public way.

L.A.M.C. Sec. 41.18 (d)
Violators are subject to prosecution

POSTED BY PROPERTY OWNER

"I USED TO LIVE IN A HOME. NOW I LIVE IN A CARDBOARD BOX." —MARY

I almost passed without noticing her, so small and still was she, sitting against the large, grey, bleak wall of the San Francisco Public Library. She seemed to be gazing at her hands, which were loosely folded in her lap. I walked back and kneeled in front of her. I told her I thought her face was beautiful and asked if I could take her photograph for this book. She smiled sadly and told me she had once been very beautiful, but that was a long time ago.

I was totally absorbed. Was it by her gentleness or her sadness or some vision of what she had lost?

She had once lived with a man who had hurt her, and she had used drugs to soothe herself. Then she lost everything.

As she told me how her life had collapsed, she began to weep. I couldn't bear to photograph her at that moment.

"THE ANGELS OF SUFFERING ARE SCREECHING AT ME!"

—DAVID

"Can't you see them? They're shooting things into my brain! They won't stop torturing me! Even in my room they don't leave me alone!"

David approached me when I was about to cross the street. Perhaps he noticed my camera and thought I was one of his tormentors, or perhaps he hoped that I knew them and could intervene on his behalf.

My first instinct was to pretend I hadn't heard him. I didn't really know what to say. In the hospital, I care for many people who say strange things. I'm not usually lost for a response, perhaps because I have some measure of control and power there. On the street, I am on *their* turf, where I feel professionally naked and where similar encounters often leave me wordless.

Before I could recover myself, he began talking volubly, with a painful intensity. His drift was difficult to follow, and it was not easy to interrupt him. When I tried, however gently, he became more agitated. At some point, not knowing what else to do, I put my hand on his arm, which seemed to calm him. There was something in his eyes that betrayed as much longing for closeness as fear of it.

He told me that he was born in Oregon to parents who separated when he was 7. He spent a confusing childhood being passed back and forth between them. At 13, he was sent to a home for juveniles, from which he regularly escaped—only to be returned each time by the police.

Defined as an adult on his 18th birthday, he was allowed to leave the facility. He had nowhere to go, so he lived on the streets in various cities. During his 20s, he became increasingly convinced that extraterrestrial creatures were shooting particles into his brain.

Currently, he lives in San Francisco, is supported by social welfare, and lives in one of the city's transient hotels. To my surprise, he agreed to let me visit him there.

His room was disheveled. In his toilet was a can of shaving cream, some of which was smeared on the mirror. He refused to allow anyone to help him clean because he didn't want strangers in his room, touching his things.

He passes his days walking around the city trying to duck the cameras he is convinced are tracking him. At times he becomes so delusional and confused that he can no longer take care of himself. When things reach this point, he is hospitalized and given medication, but as soon as he leaves the hospital, he dumps his pills down the toilet, fearing they will poison his brain. And the cycle begins again.

"IS THAT ALL YOU COULD GET ME?" — Daniel

I passed him sitting against a Walgreens drug store in the financial district, with a cigarette in his mouth. He barely responded to me other than to say that he panhandled during the day and slept in doorways at night. He also told me that he had been placed many times in the psychiatric ward of the city hospital.

He asked me to buy him a bowl of chili. When I did so and handed it to him, he looked up at me and scowled, *"Is that all you could get me?"*

I bought him another portion, which seemed to satisfy him.

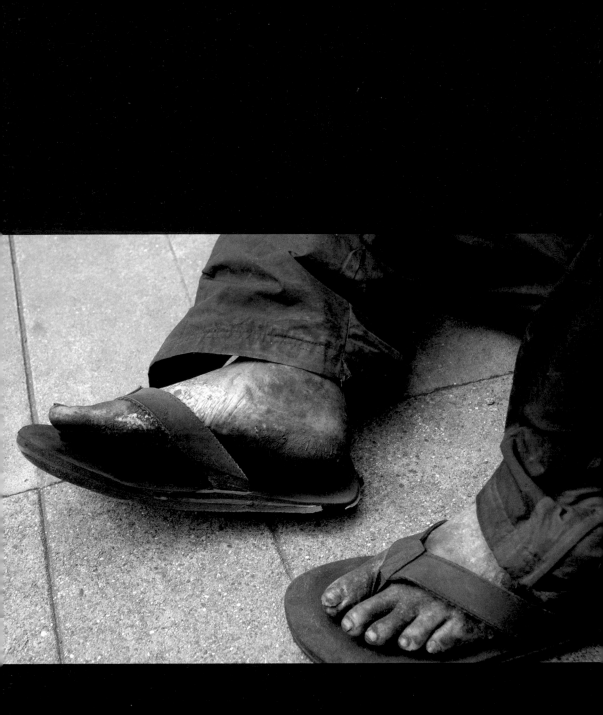

"HE NEEDS TO SEE I'VE DONE MY PENANCE." —BARBARA

"The first time I was in prison was for armed robbery when I was 15. I was completely strung out on heroin. I had rounded up two guys to help me hold up a pharmacy. The pharmacist didn't hand over the drugs right away so I aimed the gun just over his head and pulled the trigger. I didn't hit him. The other guys got caught and ratted on me. I was tried in adult court and got five years to life because I was the shooter. I was in prison for 14 months but got out on a technicality.

"I don't know when I was actually born. My mother told me 1943, but my birth certificate says 1949. My mother and father were already separated. My brother and sister and I all had different fathers. When I was two or three, my father kidnapped me and moved me around from one state to another so no one could find us. We were discovered two years later, and I was returned to my mother. I was told later that there was some suspicion that he had molested me.

"My mother had been a wild bar girl during the war. She used to tell me stories that sounded so enticing. I was her biggest fan. I followed in her footsteps because I wanted to be a character in one of her dramas. Also, I guess it was a way of staying close to her in my mind. To this day, I don't know which stories are hers and which are mine.

"When I was a teenager, I hopped freight trains and rode the rails all around the country. And then I got into crack and then into armed robberies. I was shot several times in the stomach and the legs, usually by the police. I got away with 43 burglaries, but during the 44th, I was caught and put in prison for three years.

"I met my husband when I was 25. We lived together on and off for 23 years. We had a son together. When I was delivering in the hospital, my son got stuck in the birth canal waiting for the doctor to come, and was born deaf. He wouldn't have been born at all if I hadn't grabbed the nurse by the collar and shouted at her, 'This baby's gonna die if you don't get it out!' He needed a lot of special help as a kid.

"When I was 48, my husband locked himself in the bathroom to fix and died of a heroin overdose. At the time, I had been gone for three days, strung out on crack and turning tricks to feed my habit and pay the rent. I don't know how long it took for my son to get worried enough to start banging on the door, but he couldn't get my husband to open it.

"I can't seem to forgive myself, you know, for doing something so stupid as smoking that glass prick of crack and not being there when my husband needed me and forcing my son to find him. After that, my life stopped. I lost my mind. At first I couldn't even come up with a desire to eat. I got so skinny I had to walk into a room twice to cast a shadow. I had no desire to do anything but smoke crack and use heroin because there was the chance that I might take something that wasn't survivable.

"And I was having a hard time making it home for my son, and I was sleeping in the street more and more. My son could see me from the window while I was out in the street, working. To this day, I see his face looking out the window at me, wanting me to come in. I don't know why I didn't come in for him. When he was 12, he was taken away from me and put into the foster care system. I lost track of him for years. I can't really forgive myself for making him go through all of that.

"After my son was taken, I lived out of a shopping cart. I didn't feel I had the right to come in. I wasn't really living because I didn't really want to.

"When a woman is homeless, no matter how clean she is about her person, and I was pretty clean, people can tell. I'd stop and take a whore's bath every day. I'd go to the parking garage and would wash my body and feet in the bathroom, then use the *hand drier and stuff. I kept myself in clothes that were moderately commercial, you know, and I still had my teeth at that time, but you can't really hide it when you're homeless, using, and turning tricks. And the longer I stayed strung out, the worse I looked, so it became harder and harder to make money on the street, and it took longer and longer to make. It's a story I don't like to really talk about because it took me a long time to come back from that, and I'm still coming back from it.*

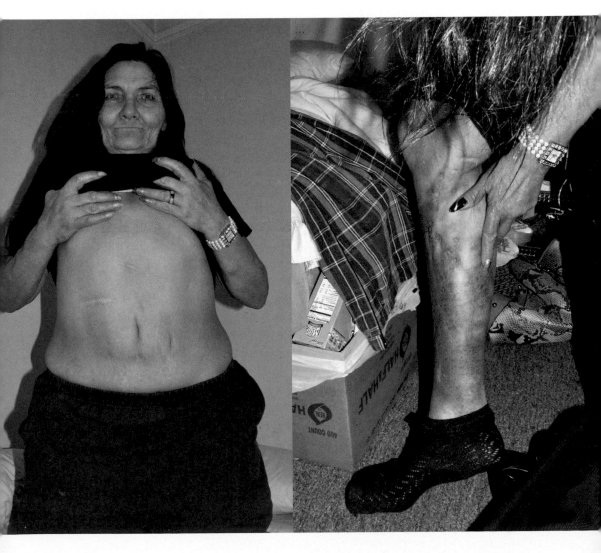

"Once, I was hospitalized on a psychiatric unit for a drug overdose, and because I was such a mess and because I was always putting myself in dangerous situations. The doctor told me I had manic depression. When I'd get depressed, I wouldn't want to live. When I got manic, I became hyper, I couldn't concentrate, couldn't live in my own skin, did crazy things.

"It was a cop who saved my life. He found me squatting in an alley with a needle in my arm. He took me to the methadone program at San Francisco General Hospital. 'This is your chance,' he told me. 'The next time, you're going to jail.' I started taking methadone and got into a case management program. My social worker helped me get meds for my manic depression, got me onto welfare, and helped me get a room. I've been clean now for five years. I eat one meal a day and live on $20 a week. Primarily, I live on cereal and maybe a sweet potato and a vegetable.

"Living in this building with so many addicts and ex-addicts is a challenge. It's hard to keep my things safe here. Either they're stolen by other clients, by the staff who have a key to my room, or by the fire department because all the papers I have here supposedly creates a fire hazard.

"One of the toughest things about my life right now is not having any teeth. When I was living on the street, I lost them all to infection. I finally got Medicaid to pay for fake ones four years ago, but they were run over by a car, only months after I had gotten them. I was getting out of a bus when someone accidentally pushed me off the last step onto the street. My jaw hit the pavement, and out jumped my teeth into the path of an oncoming car. The last I saw of them they were little white things stuck into the car's tire, rolling down the street. I have to wait another year before I can get them replaced because Medicaid will only pay for teeth once every five *years. It's not easy to eat. I chew my food the best I can and then swallow the rest whole.*

"But the worst is that I hate the way I look. I don't like smiling and I don't feel like flirting. I used to be pretty, but now when I look at myself in the mirror, I see a fat, toothless old woman.

"I still miss my husband incredibly. I still talk to him in my mind. It's been 10 years and I know it's time for me to move on, but I just can't seem to do it. I don't feel like I really deserve to bring anyone else into my life for some reason, which makes it impossible to let anyone get close to me. It's as though I'm always waiting for something, like the record button is stuck on hold.

"Maybe if my son accepted me, my life would change. I haven't seen him since he was 12. He's 20 now and in college somewhere. I lost the only photo I had of him, when I was living on the streets. I don't have his address, but I send him any extra money I have through someone who knows how to reach him. I don't think he's at the point where he really wants to see me yet. And I guess I'm afraid to see him. I've suggested meeting him a couple of times, but it never actually happened. Either he didn't make it or I didn't make it. I just want him to know I'm there for him. He needs to see I've done my penance."

I went to see Barbara in her hotel room a year after our initial conversations. She had been "graduated" from her case management program because she had been able to stabilize her life (i.e., she had a roof over her head and was no longer using drugs). She was still unable to figure out how to find her son's new contact information but told me she probably wouldn't write to him anyway, fearing he would tell her that he wanted nothing to do with her. At this point, she became tearful.

At the time of this last conversation, it was late December, and her room was so cold that both of us had to keep our winter coats on. She told me that despite four written complaints, she hadn't been able to get the hotel management to fix her radiator since it had broken down the previous winter.

When we approached the hotel manager, he could find "only" one complaint that Barbara had written eight months earlier and assumed the problem had been fixed. By the time I left, he had found an electric heater to tide her over "temporarily," although this, he informed us, was in violation of the fire code. Was he implying that he was doing Barbara a favor she should be grateful for?

I was struck by Barbara's powerlessness to get something so simple, yet so essential, addressed. Being "graduated" from her program did her no favors, as she still obviously needed the support and advocacy that it had provided her. It was just one of the many examples I encountered of health care rationing, in which one client, having become barely stable, gets pushed off the rolls in order to make way for another client who is marginally more impaired and in need of service.

A few months following my last contact with Barbara, I attempted to call her. I was told she was dead, killed by a rapidly metastasizing cancer. I never expected her to die in this way. A drug overdose after a relapse, hypothermia from exposure, perhaps infection— but not cancer.

Notwithstanding the brevity of our friendship, her death has left a noticeable hole in my heart.

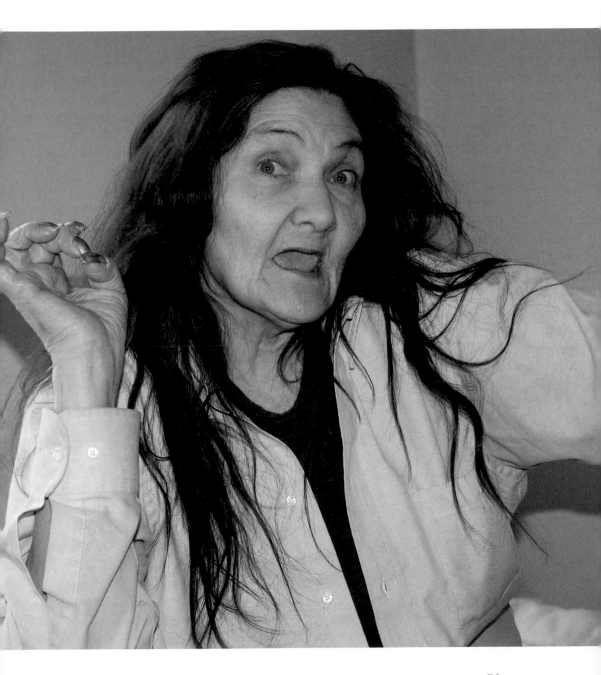

THE CHESS GAME

I played three games of chess with a man on Market Street. There were 10 other games going on simultaneously. For the price of $2, a chess board could be rented, and $5 bets placed.

My opponent was demented. He asked me what my name was after every other move and kept shouting out the date of his birth. Every few minutes, someone would irritably threaten to throw him into the traffic if he didn't "shut his fuckin' mouth." But nothing could stop the man's relentless yelling.

Every time he reached for his chess piece, his hand shook so violently that it was impossible to tell which he intended to move. Not until he had actually grasped the piece did it become clear.

In each of three games against him, I didn't last more than 12 moves. I lost $15 in a quarter of an hour.

MAN EXAMINING HIS SOCK

I sat beside him for over an hour. He seemed completely unaware of my presence, so intently was he examining his sock. When I returned two hours later, he was sitting in the same spot, still gazing at it.

"THE WORLD ENDED IN 1967, AND THERE'S NO PLACE TO GO." —MAN WITH HIS BICYCLE

I had been watching this man push his bike around the financial district on a sultry day. The bike was loaded with all his possessions. Its rear tire was flat. He sat down to drink, at which point I approached him. During the course of a short, awkward conversation, I asked him about his flat tire.

"Yea, my tire's flat. So what?"

"Wouldn't it be easier for you to push your bike if it weren't?" I suggested.

"What difference would it make? The world ended in 1967, and there's no place to go anyway," he said irritably, as though any jerk could have seen that. He waved me away.

As I turned to leave, he looked up at the sky and said philosophically, *"If it's raining, you can't fix the roof, and if it's not raining, you don't have to fix the roof."*

I met him again six months later. He looked thinner and more haggard.

"There's a guy in the city who flies around. 'Cause, you know, when you buzz a place, or how many places have you buzzed?"
"I've never buzzed anyplace."
"Well, I used to blow a helicopter."

"You used to what?"
"Well, a helicopter!"

"You flew a helicopter?"
"No, I fly a helicopter! If I had a helicopter, I'd fly out of here."

"Where would you go?"
"Out of here!"

"Yea, but do you know where you'd go?"
"I'd just fly out of here! Anywhere! 'Cause there's no airport."

I had to keep reminding myself that he was the "crazy" one, not I.

WOMAN WITH HER SLEEPING BAG —ALEXANDRA

I saw a blue sleeping bag floating down the street. I followed it
for a few minutes and watched two hands emerge and dig into a
trash can, pulling out and drinking a discarded, half-finished cup
of coffee. I maneuvered myself in front of the enshrouded figure
and asked if she wanted to go for coffee with me. She came but
was hard to engage in conversation. She told me in a flat Italian
accent that her name was Alexandra, that she had come to San
Francisco from Italy the previous year on vacation but couldn't
remember exactly where in that country she'd come from. There
was almost nothing else she could recall, except that she'd had
some kind of fall but couldn't remember where it had happened
or whether she had lost consciousness.

She said that she slept on the street and ate what people threw
away. I asked her whether she got cold at night and whether
there was anything I could do for her. She responded no and no.
She seemed totally unperturbed about her situation, including
her complete loss of recall. In fact, she said that she didn't really
want to remember anything.

She politely thanked me for the coffee and said she needed to
be on her way. I saw her a few hours later changing her shirt
in the middle of the square, totally unaware that people were
staring at her.

"I'M GONNA DIE SOONER OR LATER. I DON'T REALLY CARE WHEN. I'M TOO SAD." —TATANKA LUTA

"They call me Tatanka Luta, Alma Red Bull. I'm a Sioux warrior. I'm a very strong man. I grew up in South Dakota on a reservation, and I been stuck here since 2000. Back home, my daughter and wife died in a head-on collision."

He was crouching against a store window on Market Street when I approached him. I asked him how long ago it had happened.

"Nineteen eighty-three. My daughter, Lalita, was only three years old. Goddamn fuckin' Navajo drinking. They were going up the hill in a car, and a truck smashed into them. I was at work in the Navajo mines when it happened. It's karma. My dad got run over by a semitruck when I was three. A few years later, my mom was killed by a guy who ran into her with his car when she was crossing the street. So my whole family was totally wiped out. My whole life was wiped out.

"After my wife and daughter died, I stopped working. I stopped living. Fuck everything! I had a stereo, clothes, TV, food in the refrigerator. I said fuck it, man, I'm outta here. I took my truck and I wrecked it around and a pole. People didn't like me because I was mad, I was so mad. But you can't never be angry at God. Because things happen for a reason. I pray, I just pray, man. People try to talk to me, but I don't want to pay attention. All they say, 'We're very sorry it happened.'

"I never drank before they were killed. Now, I have to keep drinkin'. It calms my soul.

"I'm gonna die sooner or later. I don't really care when. I'm too sad. All I do is walk around by myself, try to be happy, that's all. Walk around, walk around. All night long I walk around the city. In the rain, I walk around, too. I always walk all over the place, man. I go to Two Hills to pray. I sleep in the bushes near the movie theater around here. There's more cover than on the streets. I just want to stay alone because I'm too sad. No home, no daughter, no wife. I'm still so angry, man!"

"I WAS FOUR YEARS ON DEATH ROW." —MAN WITH HIS DOG

I was walking along Haight Street in San Francisco when I saw a man with a pitbull.

"Can I take a picture of your dog?" I asked.
"Go ahead. I don't give a fuck!" he answered in a Southern drawl.

"Will he bite me if I pet him?"
"Ask him. I don't know. Sometime he do and sometime he don't. When his eyes cross, nobody know for sure."

"What's his name?
"Lipshit."

"Lipshit? Where in the world did he get that name?" I asked, laughing.
"His name used to be Nigel. He didn't answer to that. So one day I called him Lipshit. He looked up, so that's his name now. He's a hump doggin' dude," he said proudly. *"The other day, he jumped up and bit me right on my dick. Dirty Ernie. Yesterday he was on top my arm. A cop who was writin' me a ticket for drinkin' said, 'What's that dog doin'?' I said, 'He's humpin' my arm. Whatta ya think he's doin'?'"*

"How did you learn to tell such colorful stories?"
"I was four years on death row. I had a lotta time to practice." All humor was gone in an instant.

"How did you come to be on death row?"
"I caught a guy molestin' my daughter. I blew him in half with a shotgun. The state was gonna gas me, but at the last minute I got a reprieve. They decided I was crazy. I spent the next 14 years in a nut house. I'm not sure whether that were better or worse than a gassing."

"MY TWO DAUGHTERS WERE BLOWN TO BITS BY SUICIDE BOMBERS IN IRAQ." —HEIDI

I met Heidi at the Ferry Building in San Francisco. She was sitting alone on a concrete wall, holding onto a cart filled with her possessions. She related her story in a pressured, rambling, jerky manner, speaking almost inaudibly at times. I frequently had to ask her to repeat herself and often wondered whether I had missed the connection between parts of what she was saying. I have edited her narrative for the sake of coherence, but the language is hers and I haven't added anything of substance.

"I had three kids. Two were girls. Laura went into the army when she was 19 and was sent to Iraq. One year later, she was blown up by a little girl with explosives attached to her. All I have left of Laura is a flag and her rusty dog tags. There was nothing left to bury.

"I pleaded with my second daughter, Nina, to stay out of the army, but she enlisted anyway as soon as she was 18 in order to 'kick some fuckin' ass over in Iraq.' She went to revenge her sister, but as soon as she got there, she was killed by a roadside bomb. And now I have no more daughters—only a 14-year-old son who keeps telling me that he's going to go into the army 'to bring Nina and Laura home.' He's living in Nebraska with his father.

"My mother told me that I started drinking when I was a year old. My dad took care of me during the day while she worked. He put whiskey in my bottle to keep me quiet. When I was in elementary school, my teacher discovered whiskey mixed with my milk. She took it away, and I went into DTs.

"My father left my mom and me when I was five. He married someone else and never gave a penny to us. I lived with my mom

until I was about 11 and then started running away because my stepfather was molesting me. I started skipping school and not coming home at night. A judge took me away from my mom because she couldn't control me. I lived in foster homes and shelters and sometimes with my grandmother. When I was 13, I was put into juvenile homes. I was in the system for two years. It wasn't right that I should do time for being hurt by my stepfather.

"I got married when I was 15. He was 23. I managed not to get pregnant until I was 18. He kept beating me up. One day, when I was pregnant with twins, he went crazy, punched me to the floor and kicked my face with his steel-toe boots. He broke my jaw and I lost all my teeth on the right side of my mouth. I had to have my

jaw wired for months. The twins died. Then one day, I put a hard ball in a sock and beat the living shit out of him. That man never laid hands on me again. I was 21 when I got away from him.

"I've been drinking on and off for years, and now I have a bad crack habit. I've had leukemia for a long time. I don't live in a shelter because I don't want to be packed into a room with five other people. My leukemia has hurt my immune system, and God knows what diseases are running around the shelters. It's safer for me to live on the streets. I sleep near the second column under the Bay Bridge with my boyfriend, Jeff, when he's around.

"I've been going with Jeff for eight years. But he uses speed, and I never know when he'll be here and when he won't. I spend most of my time waiting for him to show up. After six hours, I go back to the Bay Bridge, pissed off, disappointed, and wondering where in the world he is and when I'm going to see him again.

"I'm pregnant now, in my first trimester. Jeff hasn't fucked me in months. My sexuality is color-coded. When I'm in a red mood, I want to be fucked long and hard. When I'm in a yellow mood, I want it soft. When I'm in a black mood, I want it fast, bang, bang, bang, and then exit. It's the way I get my anger out."

On one occasion, Heidi told me that she had missed several of her prenatal appointments at the hospital. Though I had my doubts about her "pregnancy," I urged her to keep her next appointment and told her that I'd accompany her if she wished. She agreed, but our intention was almost thwarted by not knowing what to do with her cart and its possessions. We couldn't take it on the bus, we couldn't wheel it five miles to the hospital, we couldn't find a safe place to store it, we couldn't simply leave it unattended on the street, and we couldn't initially find anyone to guard it for the afternoon.

Many physicians, including me at times, fail to recognize that patients can't get to the hospital for their appointments unless they figure out a solution to this problem. This, like so many other problems faced by homeless people, tends to be invisible from the vantage point of a traditional office setting. And on that day with Heidi, notwithstanding all my training and experience, and all the resources in the city at my disposal, I could not come up with a way of dealing with Heidi's cart, short of guarding it myself while she went to her appointment. Just as I was about to suggest this, one of her acquaintances appeared; this person was willing, for a few dollars, to look after her cart. Gratefully, we got on the next bus and rode to the hospital, only to discover that the doctor had been called away on an emergency and the clinic was closed. Back we went to retrieve her cart three hours later.

One of the last times I saw Heidi, I almost failed to recognize her. She was dressed in leggings, black shorts, and a red blouse, her hair pulled into pigtails. She was wearing lipstick, mascara, and a sweet-smelling perfume. She told me she had been made up by a cosmetics clerk at a nearby store who wanted to help her "get her man back." She had been waiting for Jeff in the hot sun all day, dressed in this outfit. When she finally realized that he wasn't going to show, she crumpled in disappointment and sobbed.

"WELL, I DON'T KNOW WHAT ROCK BOTTOM IS, IF THIS ISN'T IT. I HAVE NOTHING LEFT!" —RYAN

"I'm on a five-day speed run. I haven't slept for two or three days. I can hardly think straight.

"I have a bad, bad habit. Just the word 'speed' sets me off. It has me so bad. So bad. When I just think about the meth getting into my blood, I start sweating I want it so much. No one can stop me if I have a mind to use. And once I start, I can't stop. It's so hard to get off. I'm too weak. And I can always get it, even when I don't have any money. Dealers give it to me free because I bring them customers, my friends. I call them my friends, but you know what? They're not. The only thing that helps me is pot. It helps my craving for a while. But the craving always comes back.

"People say, 'Well, you haven't hit rock bottom yet.' And I say, 'Well, I don't know what rock bottom is, if this isn't it. I have nothing left!' My friend died from a brain aneurysm he got from speed, man. I see what it can do to you, and I still can't stop. Sometimes I think I'll only stop using when I'm dead.

"You know what? All the services I'm offered, I blow. A program is only going to work for someone who wants it. If you have any kind of ambivalence, it's not going to work. I know this is fucked up, but I need a reason to stop. I need a person in my life. I need something to pull me in a positive direction. But no one's going to save my life. I've got to do it.

"Sex is a big part of it. You could put a wig on a pig, and I'd go after it when I'm on speed. It just makes all your fantasies come true. That's the hardest part to give up. I have all kinds of sexual fantasies, mostly about older women, incest. I don't want to talk

about it. I had a fucked-up childhood, babysitters and shit. Meth makes your body feel so good. Think of the best orgasm you ever had and multiply it times 1,000. When I'm on a run, I want to fuck, fuck, fuck. Even after you come, your body still feels wonderful. I sometimes fuck for 15 hours. I'm a freak when I'm on meth.

"I'm also addicted to women. I gotta have them. That's probably why I did [i.e., initiated into drugs] *my girlfriend, Crystal. Her ex-boyfriend did me. I did her. I'm sick, in my head. I put a needle in her arm and got her addicted to meth. That's the worst thing I ever did in my life. She had had some argument with her dad, and she pleaded, 'Give me some.' 'Crystal, no, no!' I said. 'Give me some!' 'No, No!' She kept going on and on. And finally I said, 'Shut your fuckin' mouth. Here.' And I ended up putting it in her. But I never wanted to hurt her—never, never. She was my first love. I was truly in love with her for three years. And you know what makes it even worse? The first 18 months we were together, she helped me stay clean and sober, and this is how I paid her back!*

"I used to be a real scumbag. I was stealing cars as soon as I learned to drive. I'd take the coat off your back. If you let me into your house, I'd steal your suit. I've burned the hand. But that was in the past—six years ago.

"I'm not going to lie. For a time I was doing a lot of shoplifting, but I don't do it anymore. I haven't stole. I don't do shady or underhanded shit anymore. I've been in prison twice either for selling drugs or violating my parole. Prison's a blessing in disguise. It's sad, but it's the only thing that gets me off meth. In reality, you can do just as much drugs inside as you can outside, but when I'm inside, I don't do it 'cause I don't want to get caught. But prison only takes me so far 'cause I start using again the day I get out. And I can see how easy it is to get into the prison lifestyle,

'cause you don't have to take responsibility for anything. All your food, all your clothing, everything is given to you. It's easy. You know what's hard? Keeping a job, feeding your family. That is hard as fuck!

"My dad was strung out on China White [a form of heroin] for years when I was a kid. He'd make up reasons to beat the shit out of my mother and me. When he didn't have a drink, he got worse. My mother used to run to a battered women's shelter and take me with her. Then my parents split, and when I was a teenager I lived in group homes. But I had a hard time there, and I got hospitalized on psych units a few times. Every time I went in, they'd give me a new med. One time I was on 13 different meds: Haldol, Mellaril, lithium, Tegretol. I was like a zombie. I can't tell you what helped and what didn't because I was on so many at one time. I know I need meds. I know I'm manic-depressive.

"I'm gonna make it out. I already know it—just like my dad did, when he found God. He's totally changed. He really apologized to me. We're trying to patch things up between us. I know I'm gonna make it. The Lord's on my side. I just need to quit. I just need some kind of medication that blocks the speed. I just need a person in my life. Maybe if I have kids, it will straighten me out. I'm gonna get out of this."

Ryan talked nonstop for an hour, barely pausing to catch his breath. His words tumbled out with speed and intensity. There was something incredibly sweet and naïve about him, a totally lost little boy.

"SOMETIMES I GET TIRED OF HAVING A ROOF OVER MY HEAD." —LINDA

"My name is Linda. I'm living outside the bus terminal. My buddy and I take turns sleeping. I sleep with one eye open because my entire net worth is in this cart. But I'm not really a down-and-out tramp. I get SSI. Every once in a while, when I get tired of living on the streets, shit, I just give up and go live in a cheap hotel.

"But those places are depressing. They throw you in one of those tiny rooms and make you fend for yourself with the crazies and the dopers. After a while, I get sick of all of it. I get tired of having a roof over my head. Sometimes, even when it's winter, I have to get out. I can't take it no more in my room—too depressing. All I was doing was staring at the four walls listening to my nutty neighbors going off. What kind of fun is that? So I decide to hit the streets and be happy instead of being in a room with a bunch of crazies nearby and be miserable. This is more freedom to me, pushing this cart and having a little money to last as long as it does.

"Also there's the rent. I been hearing on the radio they want to cut my $960 SSI check. How much more can they cut? I can't afford rent as it is now. Hell, man, the cheapest hotel room is $700 a month. So after you pay your rent, what are you going to have left over for yourself? Same reason I don't buy gloves. It's cold out, but I'm not goin' to waste my money on gloves. You know what I'm saying? If I spent money on rent and gloves, I couldn't afford something like these gangster headphones and this watch. This watch makes me happy every time I look at it. It kind of reminds me that I'm not a total failure, else I wouldn't have it.

"To me, I have money today, I better spend it, because tomorrow I may not be here, you know what I'm sayin'? I don't know, man, I

might get mugged, might get hit by a car. I've always lived day to day ever since I can remember.

"I had a hard life growing up in Chicago. My parents supposedly broke my arm and burned my feet in the fire when I was a kid. Family services took me away from them when I was five or

something. I wish I could remember all that. I don't even know who the hell they were. I been through so many foster parents, more than 10, you know, so to be honest with you, I can't remember what my real parents looked like.

"I was a problem child. I couldn't concentrate in school. I was always throwing fits and acting up. Nobody seemed to know what the problem was. These foster parents always said they didn't know how to handle me. I don't know what you call it in the foster care business. Undesirable? So I ended being raised up in group homes and institutions.

"After I got out of school, I could never hold down a job for too long, and that's how I got to living on the streets. Then I started thinking crazy shit that I couldn't get out of my mind. Once I went to Safeway and told them I had a bomb in my suitcase, and they called the police. I knew I didn't have a bomb, but I just wanted to get off the streets, man. You know. I waited for the police and everything. They gave me 16 months for that.

"Sometimes I break windows or get so mad I get out of control. Whenever there is too much pressure, that's what happens. I haven't done that in a long time 'cause I learned my lesson. You go crazy on the streets and then, when you're taken to jail, they fuckin' torture you and kick the shit out of you. I'm talkin' about the guards. They got worse torture in jail than in the so-called torture camps that Uncle Sam has, man. They beat the shit out of me in jail. I'm still hurtin' from that beating. You see my thumb? It's still broken from what the guards did to it. That's how it got fucked up. All because I went off, and wasn't getting the right psychiatric help and medicine. Jail is no place for someone with mental problems. They don't give a fuck.

"The mental health system never helped me either. They said I was paranoid schizophrenic. Once I was hospitalized in the psychiatric unit, the doctor gave me medicine. I call it dope. It fucks your dick up, man. You can't get your jollies off when you're on that crap. The doctor didn't even tell me what it was going to do to me. They don't tell you shit no more, man. They just give you that crap, and that's it. I went to beat my meat, you know, do my thing, and nothing came out. 'What the hell?' I said. 'I'm not taking this!'

"When I got out of the hospital, I got a social worker, but he gave up on me because I didn't go to his damn program. It reminded me too much of the group homes I had been cooped up in when I was a kid. When you get out, you tell yourself, 'I can do what I want now. I don't have to go to these places.'

"I'm still tryin' to figure out what I'm supposed to have learned from my life and all. Mostly I try to work it out by myself, because there's no one I'm really close to. I'm what you call a loner—not because I want to be. Because that's the way I was raised. When you ain't learned how to love, when you ain't learned how to be close to somebody, basically you're cooked. If you had parents that were breaking your arms, putting your feet in the fire, there's not much you're going to learn. 'Cept for don't get too close to people. You never know what they're going to do.

"I've always been shy anyway. It's probably why I don't have AIDS. I never had a relationship. No sex, no diseases. Worked out good, but then again, that loneliness can kill you, too. When I get too lonely, which is all the time, I listen to music. Can't live without it. Every time I get homeless, I always got some music with me. That's my medicine, you know.

"Sometimes the music makes me sad, but I haven't cried in a long time. The last time, I was sitting in a hotel, thinking about my mother—or at least tryin' to remember what she looked like. Usually everybody remembers what their parents were like. I don't. I was always different. I'm a transgender. I don't understand why. I was just born that way, wanting to put on a dress. But I'm not getting my dick cut off. I play both worlds."

As I was packing up my camera, I asked him how he chose to call himself Linda. *"It was my mother's name,"* he replied. *"At least I know that about her."*

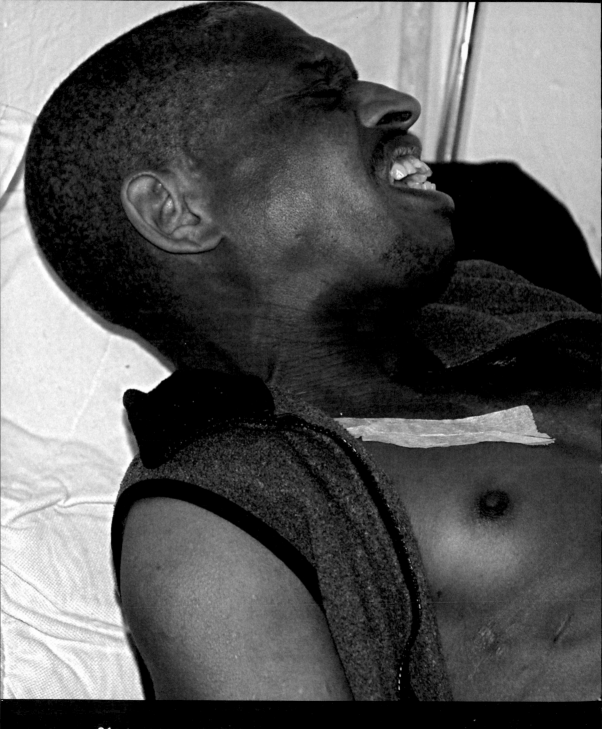

"I'VE TRADED MY PAIN MEDICATION AWAY FOR CRACK."

—GREGG

"I've had sickle cell anemia since I was a boy. I've had hundreds of sickle cell crises since then. They're incredibly painful. They've destroyed the bone in my leg and blinded me in one eye. Sometimes I don't have my pain medication when I need it 'cause I've traded it away for crack."

I met Gregg at a point when he was using crack and other drugs despite having recently obtained housing. He was being seen weekly by a social worker, who helped him with the concrete problems in his life. Crack often precipitated his sickle cell crises. He had an extreme and contorted limp, requiring that he use a cane to walk.

A few months after I met him, he was drawn into an altercation with someone who called him a "nigger" and then attacked him. Gregg struck back with his cane in self-defense. Apprehended by the police, who didn't believe his side of the story, Gregg was sentenced to house arrest for three months and monitored with an electronic collar attached to his ankle. He was also required to attend a drug treatment program and to undergo random drug screens. It was only at this point that he stopped using drugs, whereupon the frequency of his sickle cell crises decreased substantially.

Gregg's early life had been complicated. After he was diagnosed with sickle cell anemia as a boy, his father left the family. His mother, soon after, developed a relationship with a married man who supported her and her six children while he continued to live with his wife. One day when Gregg was an adolescent, he walked in on his mother smoking crack with some of her friends. He thought,

"Man, that looks great," and with the encouragement of his older brother, he began using it himself. Over time, he developed a network of friends with whom he smoked, stole, and fought to support his habit.

Gregg's life is a testimony to the compulsive power of crack. When he was stoned, he maintained a cheerful, optimistic, charming bravado that hid his discouragement and sense of defeat. When he didn't have crack, he became a totally different person—desperate and unreachable. From his early 20s, crack had sabotaged his ability to work; drove him into the streets, where he lived for years; destroyed important relationships; led to multiple incarcerations; and regularly provoked extremely painful sickle cell crises.

These crises destroyed the bone in his leg and required the surgical removal of his left eye, but even this and the intense pain of his crises couldn't compete with his addiction. When the pain became too severe, he'd call an ambulance and be taken to the city hospital's emergency room, where he'd be given a small quantity of pain medication to get him through the episode. After several days, he'd feel better, go out to the street, hustle for money and drugs, and start the cycle all over again.

I found myself in an internal struggle, blaming Gregg for some of the misery of his life on the one hand, and recognizing how totally out of control he was on the other. The power of his addiction and his inability to resist it, despite the fact that it was eating away at his body and slowly killing him, took my breath away.

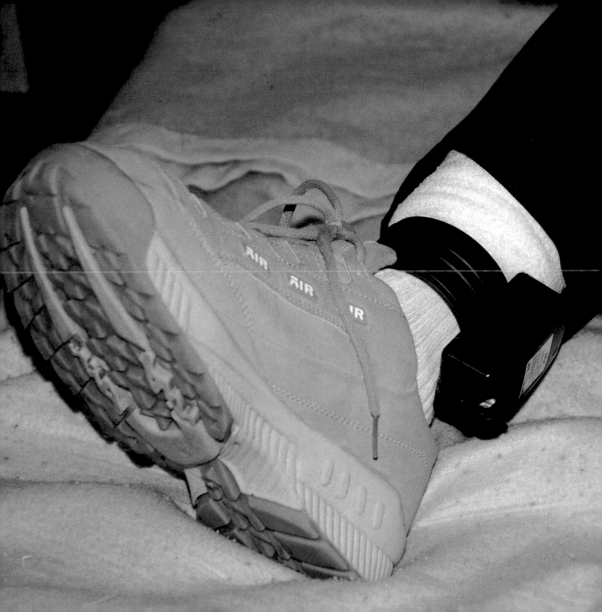

"I'M SURE MY MOM DIDN'T WANT TO GIVE ME AWAY."

—MAN WITH HIS DAFFY TIE

"I'm letting them know that their pyramid scheme is bullshit, because the human condition won't allow it. Thanks, asshole. Whoever was behind me, thank you, I'll clean up your dog shit now. Well, somebody's got to do it."

I heard Rick before I saw him, talking truculently to himself and to everyone who passed. People stepped around him on the path. He eventually came over to where I was sitting and began talking angrily about "assholes, motherfuckers from foreign countries who are trying to steal everything we have." He was pressured and enraged during most of our conversation, and I was able to interrupt him only with the greatest care and deference.

He told me that he had been living on the street for years, had been incarcerated several times for drug possession, had passed through various drug treatment programs, and was thrown out of the last one two years earlier for refusing to take a urine test.

When he began talking about his parents, he began to cry. *"I miss my mother, man. See, she had me from somebody I never met. My mother, she had to give me away to the court when I was 14. I got in trouble with the authorities. Then it was group homes, state raised, ward of the court. I'm sure my mom didn't want to give me away. It was just she couldn't handle me. I don't blame her. I don't hate her. I'm not mad at her. She didn't know any better. She had a hard life, man. She's been duped by her own life. It causes her pain to see me, so I keep away. I'm going to get a truck and live in the mountains like my father did."*

"I FELL FROM THE EMPIRE STATE BUILDING TO THE CURB."

—BRIDGETT

"I met my husband when I was 20. He was dealing and using cocaine. Everyone wanted to talk to him, and I thought that he was very impressive. We lived in Los Gatos in a real nice house and had beautiful cars and three great kids. We both had good jobs. We were both raking in the money. I was working as an account manager, overseeing a million-dollar account. Everything was really good.

"When I was in my early 30s, my husband had an affair with our nanny and things changed. I started to drink. Then one night he hit me and knocked me unconscious onto the kitchen table. I had Chloe, my youngest, in my arms at the time.

"'I'm leaving,' I said. I took Chloe, and he took the boys. Even though I was drinking, I was a very functional alcoholic. I was never the type that passed out on the sofa. I drank when my kids went to bed. I drank at lunch meetings. But no one could ever tell. I was doing good. I still had a job. I had a nice, beautiful penthouse apartment and a new BMW.

"Chloe was very feminine, just like her mom. She had hair down to her waist when she was four. And I used to put it up in a bun every morning. I would put music on in the bathroom, put candles on the bathtub, do her hair up for her—young lady growing up. I was a wonderful mom.

"One night I came home from a trip, and Chloe told me that my husband's brother had raped her in the butt. Chloe was four at the time, and immediately after it happened, he disappeared and was found 40 days later hanging from a tree. If he hadn't hung

himself, I would have killed him! My husband pressured me into not telling anyone. But the day that happened, my life stopped, like my soul broke down.

"I can't really remember clearly, but something like that had happened to me when I was young, too. My aunt told me that my biological father molested me when I was a very little girl. My mother and father separated after that, and my mother married my stepfather. We lived in a nice house. But my mother was a raging alcoholic, so I swore I would never, never drink. 'You're not going to be a woman like your mother,' I always told myself. My stepdad was always angry at me. He wasn't an alcoholic, but he drank to get wasted. To this day, he has a serious temper problem.

"There was always a lot of conflict between my parents: two-by-fours flying through the house, things like that. Breakfast wasn't right, plates going through the kitchen. When I was five, my half-sister was born. We never got along. I had loved being an only child. We lived above a bar. I'd climb downstairs, sit on the barstool, and I'd have Coke® and peanuts for breakfast, get a silver dollar. I was pretty damn happy. I was like the mascot of the bar. People loved to look at me. I was very talented. I was a gymnast, doing flips off the roof from when I was two and a half.

"When I was 15, my mother and stepdad separated, and I moved to Wyoming with my mom. She got into another relationship. One day she said, 'We're moving to Montana. This relationship I'm in is too violent.' I told her, 'I'm not going. I have a boyfriend. And you don't have anyplace for me to live.' She left anyway so I stayed with my boyfriend's grandparents, who kind of became my family for a while. Life was really good then. I missed school a lot but I wrote my own notes excusing my absences. Basically my mother deserted me, but my life was better without her.

"After Chloe was raped, I kept thinking about my childhood and how confusing and lonely parts of it had been. I got depressed and was crying a lot. I began to drink more and more. I couldn't fit a wine bottle into my purse, so I started drinking hard liquor, and I could drink all day. I lost my job and my house. I finally went to a residential rehab program because I was tired of hearing about my drinking from my husband, and besides, I didn't have anyplace else to go. I left Chloe with my husband, but I never went back to get her because I was living in my car. How could I take care of her if I didn't have a place? And then I drank even more. I was like counting on the alcohol. I wanted to forget what had happened to Chloe, and everything else. Also, after I left my husband, I had a boyfriend who beat me almost to death.

"I went to jail once, supposedly because I was on drugs when I was taking Chloe out for a visit. It was totally unfair. I pled guilty to child endangerment in order to reduce my sentence. I spent a whole month in jail until I thought I was going to go crazy. Jail was terrible. It was the worst thing I ever saw in my life. I couldn't even eat. I got there and I threw away my food. I thought someone was going to kill me over a piece of bread.

"After I got out, I went into a program, but I couldn't stand it there. I wanted to drink, and besides, I thought, what had my life come to if I needed an alcohol rehab program? So I moved to San Francisco. I lived in cheap hotels. I didn't see my kids at this time because I couldn't take them to a place like that. I was in shock about where my life had gone. I tried to kill myself with Xanax® and alcohol, but I woke up in the bushes with leaves in my hair. My tolerance was too high. I didn't know where to turn. And I still didn't think I had a problem. I didn't know you couldn't go through deaths, divorce, moving, jail and survive it without any help.

"I had to do something, so I got a job at a jewelry store. I made the best sale of the year. I sold a two-carat diamond. I got to wear all the jewelry I wanted. I got to wear flashy clothes. But I didn't stay there long because I broke my ankle. I was wearing high heels, and I slipped off the curb. I was taken to the hospital and then was referred to the welfare office. While I was there, I met a guy who said, 'Hey, we're having a party at the beach. Why don't you come out?' I said, 'Sure,' even though my leg was casted and I was drinking pretty bad. Then some guy, who had blown up a post office and had spent time in prison, picked me up and took me up to the hills overlooking San Francisco. We lived there for weeks. We would barbecue up there. We came down every few days to take a shower. So we didn't look like we were homeless.

"We would go downtown to eat at St. Anthony's soup kitchen. One day, my wallet got lifted off me. I had it sticking out of my jacket. It had all of our money and food stamps. My boyfriend was so furious, he kicked out a pawnshop window. The whole window came crashing down. We ran and we never got caught. We were like Bonnie and Clyde. We started living in an old army bunker in the cliffs above the beach. You had to climb over the seawall and then scale down about 50 feet, and then jump and roll the other 150 feet to get to it. It was mostly great, but there were mice around that were always disturbing us at night. And I got pneumonia several times from living on the beach.

"Then one day I started feeling really bad. I was getting the shakes, and I was hungry. We went to a very fancy restaurant and ordered the best food and the best bottles of wine on the menu and then disappeared before the check came. We said to each other, 'If we're going to do this, let's do it right.' I had my hair up and blue lipstick on, and the waiter never suspected anything. But soon afterwards, my boyfriend fell off the cliff we were living on and died.

"I had nowhere to go, but his best friend took me in for a while. Unfortunately, he was like some of the men my mother had. He ended up beating my face with a 40-ounce beer bottle and choked me almost to death. I finally got away and was taken to the hospital, and he was arrested and sentenced for five years. After that I went to an alcohol detox program, then worked for the Salvation Army on weekends. So I had enough to live on.

"Then I met a multimillionaire. He was a body builder. He could stop a bus in the middle of the street. People were afraid of him. And I loved it, because he talked to me so sweetly. I never had to worry for a minute. He treated me like a princess. He gave me everything I wanted. If I liked a pair of pants, he'd say, 'Well, buy three pairs.' And if I wanted Godiva® chocolates, okay. He sent me roses that were four feet tall. I'd never been happier in my life. And I was making good money again. But then he started talking about marriage, and his mother opposed it. This big-assed body builder turned out to be a squeak, totally under the thumb of his mother, and he dumped me. While we were going together, I was clean and sober for a couple of years, but then I started taking crack and drinking again.

"I've been to detox so many times, but I never stay more than a day. I hate being there. I feel like I'm being institutionalized. The staff are so pretentious. They haven't even been to college. They're ex-addicts and they think they know something. They have no clue. They've never even been outside of San Francisco in their lives. Working in a rehab program is the highest they're ever going to go. In one program, a staff member took me to a part of the house that no one knew about and thought it would be a pretty good idea to have sex. Can you believe it? And the program in San Francisco doesn't even feed you right. You can't even get real food there. All they give you is tofu and vegetarian meals, and I hate tofu.

"Four years ago, I got hooked up with the city hospital's case management program. I've been with it since then. My social worker, Lisa, is wonderful. She's the one who got me this beautiful room. I see her every other week and I'm doing much better, but I'm still drinking—minimally, but I don't get drunk. I don't go to bars. I drink in my room. I don't think most people would know I'm drinking.

"Maybe I have to go back to detox to get the alcohol completely out of my system. Maybe I'll drag myself through detox one more time, and bring my food with me this time. I should go, but I can't really do it yet, because I have no one to take care of my cat. I don't have any friends. I used to have a few friends, but they turned out to be drug addicts.

"Chloe is 16 now. She never talks about the rape. Before it, she dressed very feminine. After it, she only wore boys' clothing. That's what she wears now. She dresses very asymmetrical. She won't wear girls' clothing. She's into baseball, football, basketball. She's not feminine whatsoever. She won't talk to me. She and my boys live with their dad.

"A few years ago, I developed lupus, an autoimmune disease. My joints are always painful. I have to take 500 milligrams of morphine a day just to walk. That's how bad the pain is. They drained my knee six times last month. And a few months ago, my computer was stolen. I was starting to write children's books, and all my material was on my computer. So I don't really have much hope for the future. Actually, I don't think about it. I'm too sad. I just think about how I'm going to manage this afternoon. I worry about the TV going out."

I saw Bridgett two months later. She had gone to an alcohol detox program in the interval and was noticeably different— calmer, more logical, more reflective, and able to think more clearly about her future. But when I met with her again nine months after this, she had relapsed. She was stylishly dressed but volatile, she was slurring her words, and she nearly tripped when serving me coffee in her room. She tearfully told me the following, which I have edited for greater coherence:

"A few weeks ago, I went to a party and got a massage from a professional masseur. I suddenly woke up on the massage table and realized the masseur was sodomizing me. I jumped up and screamed that I was being raped. I didn't press charges because no one would have believed me. I started drinking again the next day.

"A week ago, I went to a counselor to talk about the rape. I came home so upset that I felt like cutting my wrists. I told my neighbor, who called the apartment manager, who came to check on me. I didn't want her in my apartment and when she wouldn't leave, I pushed her out. The apartment management company has just filed papers to have me evicted for assault. So now I am going to lose my apartment. None of this was my fault."

Bridgett also told me that she had lost her cell phone and was now cut off from telephone contact with the outside world. She said she knew she needed to go to alcohol rehab, but it was impossible to make contact with the program without a phone. Besides, there was no one to take care of her cat. And moreover, she said, she couldn't go into a program before her eviction papers were served, which could take up to six months. She could find no way around these obstacles, and whatever solutions I offered, she found reasons that none of them could work.

Six months later, I received a call that Bridgett had died of alcohol poisoning. She had been drinking very heavily for several months, developed pneumonia, left the hospital against medical advice, and was subsequently seen wandering around nude in her apartment building. The social worker from her case management program stayed in touch with her but was helpless to convince her to admit herself to an alcoholic rehab program. The mental health commitment laws made it impossible for Bridgett to be forced into treatment against her will. While an obvious and severe danger to herself, the danger was not considered "imminent," as the law requires for involuntary hospitalization.

One night she accompanied a stranger to his apartment, where they spent the night drinking heavily. He awoke the next morning to find her dead. Her body was already cold.

"ONE DAY YOU'RE GOING TO KILL ME!" —JAMES

"I'm 62 years old. I was born in Louisiana. I saw a lot of action in Vietnam. I saw my close friends killed. And I killed men. It was too much.

"When I came back to the United States, I came back to my wife. She was Philippine, but to me she looked Vietnamese. I'd wake up in the middle of the night thinking she was trying to kill me. Once I beat her up real bad. I didn't know what I was doing. She kept yelling, 'Honey, it's me! It's me!' But I couldn't hear her. One day she said to me, 'I love you, honey, but I can't stay here anymore. One day you're going to kill me!'

"The government said I had schizophrenia because it didn't want to pay for me. It said I had it before I went to Vietnam, so they weren't responsible. But my lawyer said I had traumatic disorder that developed during the war and that the government was responsible. I finally won the case. I am living in one room in this shitty building, getting SSI.

"I was in the VA hospital psychiatry ward several times. I was also in jail. I lost too many friends in the war. It gets to you. I keep thinking about it. Can't get it out of my mind. I hear voices, but I can't tell what they're saying."

"I'M IMMUNE TO PAIN IN MY BODY, BUT WHEN SOMEONE HURTS MY FEELINGS, IT MAKES ME FEEL REAL SAD AND I CRY." —ERRADYSE

I came upon Erradyse in Golden Gate Park. She was sitting on the grass. I told her I thought her fur coat looked terrific and was rewarded with a beautiful smile.

"I have to buy myself some new pants, with fishnet, because I've had these pants on for months. And I gotta get my coat cleaned. My coat keeps me warm. I mostly live outside. I can stay indoors for four or five days, and then I have to come out, else I'll die. I die inside. My lungs slow down. I stay in a camper or a van. Sometimes I'm in the hospital and sometimes in jail. And then I have to get out, because if I stay there my veins, my blood cells break and multiply. When I live outside, I start to feel better because I get more oxygen. When it's cold and windy and rainy, I don't get cold. I'm immune to the weather, even in the cold and the rain. I love the outdoors. I survive out here, with the oxygen.

"I don't do drugs or alcohol, so it's not expensive to live. I'm on welfare. Sometimes I beg cigarettes and food. When I'm selling sex, I only ask one time. They say no, I walk away. I don't beg. I charge $40 on up for half and half—suck their dick until it gets hard, and then let them fuck me. In my asshole, it's $60.

"I want the man to stay in me, but they don't. I guess they don't want me to have their baby. I usually tell black men to put a condom on, 'cause I don't want them to think I'm trying to get child support from them, so I mention condom first. Usually they don't want to use no condom. I don't know how their sperm stays inside of me, but it does. My vagina sucks the sperm out of

the man's dick and don't release it. What kinda animal is that? What kinda animal has sex, and the sperm doesn't come out for months and years? It never comes out. It goes into the wall near my ovaries. And then it dies, but it still sits there.

"I've been in San Francisco since 1982. I'm 45 years old. I go to the clinic and get checks up. If I get AIDS, I'll get a blood transfusion. They'll take all my blood out, and they'll put new blood in. Then I'll sweat through my pores. Stay in the hospital for a couple of months. My Medi-Cal will pay for that.

"I got to get this bruise under my eye cleaned. A white girl be disrespecting me. I get in her face. She say, 'Get out of my face.' I say, 'No!' Then we fight, and a man get involved. He punched me. She kicked me all over. It didn't hurt. I don't know why. I'm immune to pain in my body, but when someone hurts my feelings, it makes me feel real sad and I cry. White girls say, 'Get off the street. You can't have no white man. Fuck black men. Don't fuck white men.' They don't want me around. I don't know why they care who's fucking me."

"IF YOU HAVE NO TEETH, IT'S PROOF THAT YOU'VE FUCKED UP REAL BAD—THAT YOU MUST BE NOTHING BUT A FUCK-UP!" —JEFF

"I turn away and cover my mouth when a woman smiles at me. She'd never look at me again if she saw I had no teeth. Even if I got dentures, it wouldn't help, because it's not goin' to fool her. As soon as we kissed, she'd realize it. She'd be completely disgusted and think I'd misled her. She'd drop me like a hot potato. Better not to let anything start. It would be too painful. I've been telling myself, 'Quit looking at women. You're just torturing yourself. It's not gonna happen! You're gonna be alone all your life. It's wicked sad, but that's the way it is.' I'm doomed.

"If you have a big nose, well, no one can blame you. It's just the way you were born. But if you have no teeth, it's proof that you've fucked up real bad—that you must be nothing but a fuck-up!"

Jeff was referred to me by a case management program at San Francisco General Hospital. Shortly before I met him, he had been using drugs heavily and had been living on the street.

"My life didn't start out so good. My mother went nuts when I was five. She heard voices, and was in and out of mental hospitals. Everybody in the neighborhood knew she was crazy. She wouldn't let me have friends over to the house because she was a neat freak and was afraid they'd mess up the house. She always was calling me a 'no good son of a bitch.' Sometimes she'd take after my father with a knife. I was always afraid she'd kill me.

"My sister ran away from home when I was six. My parents sent me out to find her, but it was hopeless. We never heard from her again. My parents were totally indifferent.

"My father was my hero. He was a garbage collector—the best in the city. He never even left a gum wrapper on the ground. I became a garbage collector, too. I worked and paid taxes for 12 years. But one day I was caught with a tiny bit of pot in my urine and was fired on the spot. It was ridiculous!

"Being a garbage man was everything to me. When I lost that, I lost everything! I got so depressed I could barely get out of bed. One day I started using crack, and then heroin. In no time I burned through all my money, lost my apartment, and lost my connection to my family. I also lost my fiancée, but I suppose I didn't deserve her anyway. I was nothing but a worthless piece of shit.

"For the next 10 years, I slept over a heating vent on the sidewalk. When it rained, I'd hop onto someone's porch to stay dry. Living on the street is so bad, you have to be either stoned or crazy to bear it. And San Francisco is a fuckin' cold, foggy city.

"During those years, I nearly died a couple of times from overdoses. I couldn't get through a day without a fix; I'd get real sick. When you're on heroin, you just can't let that happen. You'll do anything to prevent it. You can't think of anything except drugs and trying to stay alive. I tried panhandling in the early days, but that takes too much patience and is completely unreliable. Even in the best of days, it doesn't pay enough for your heroin. Most days, if you got $10 panhandling, you were lucky. I supported my habit by shoplifting. I'd go into stores, stuff four bottles of wine worth $100 in my jacket, and then fence them all for $40. I probably shoplifted $200,000 of wine altogether in those years. Can you fuckin' believe it, man? I was caught and arrested 53 times, but the San Francisco jails are so full that I only spent a total of 30 days in jail. The police usually just gave me a warrant and let me go—until the last time, when I was nearly sentenced for a year.

"Lots of times, when everyone else in the city was sleeping, I'd stay up all night, stoned on crack, and walk the streets looking for money that people had dropped. It's amazing how much I'd find. The other thing I'd do was sell my food stamps. It's illegal, but there's a whole industry run by little old Chinese ladies called mama-sans, who will buy your $80 of food stamps for $40. The police know about them, but they don't do anything. 'Let them have their measly 40 bucks,' they say. 'It's theirs anyway. If they don't get it this way, they'll steal it and we'll pay the price in more police calls.'

"I never spent my money on a room, even when it was freezing outside. Six hundred dollars a month for a crappy, little, dark room with no kitchen and no bathroom? No fuckin' way! I preferred to use my money for drugs, and sleep on the street rather than waste it on a miserable place like that!

"Shelters are just as bad, but in a different way. I never spent a night in one. They're dangerous and crowded. You're always sleeping with someone's smelly feet in your face, and someone else breathing up your nose. I was afraid I'd catch some disease there.

"Last year, my skin and one of my teeth got infected. I got abscesses all over my body. They wouldn't heal while I was on the street, even with antibiotics. Too much stress, too much exposure to bad weather, too many heroin injections. The bacteria spread to my heart and nearly killed me. I was in the city hospital for 133 days on IV antibiotics. It cost the city over thousands of dollars! I agreed to let the dentist pull all my teeth so they wouldn't get reinfected and kill me for good next time.

"On account of I cost the city so much money, I was referred to a methadone treatment program and then to a special program for people who cost the city a lot of money in medical care. I got hooked up with Lisa, a social worker, who saw me every day for a year. She's an angel. She bailed my ass out of jail when I was facing a one-year prison term. She got me onto welfare, helped me find a rent-subsidized apartment, and was the reason I gave up drugs. It's really embarrassing, but I fell completely in love with her. One day, I just quit using because I couldn't look her in the face anymore after all she had done for me. It's totally corny, but it was the only way I could show her what she meant to me. If it weren't for Lisa, I'd be dead.

"I've been clean for six months now, the first time in 10 years. I've started volunteering at an animal shelter 'cause I'm getting sick of doing nothing except watching TV. I also adopted this neat little kitten. She's my best friend. I've also started to think about what else I want to do with my life. Maybe I'll live 'til 50."

I saw Jeff six months after this last conversation. He was still free of drugs and had begun working as a paid, part-time administrative staff member in the program that had saved his life.

"I DON'T SLEEP. I DON'T EAT." —MICHAEL

At first I thought I was looking at a bundle of rags. But then it moved, and I saw a pair of eyes peeking out from behind a hood. As I turned to him, he began talking softly to himself and then more loudly to the bell that clanged in the tower of the Ferry Building at 15-minute intervals.

"Who are you talking to?" I asked him.
"God," he responded.
"How do you get in touch with him?" I pursued.
"Through the bell," he whispered, and abruptly stood up and walked away, pushing his cart in front of him.

I saw him again a few days later, when he was more loquacious.

"I'm a Jehovah's Witness. I wrote an art book. You can look it up in the Library of Congress."

"I went to barber school and learned to grow women's hair. I don't cut it, I grow it."

"I was born in DC, and I never left. And I'm never going to leave. I walked from DC to San Francisco. It took me a few weeks."

"Last night I slept with my wife. She sleeps in Israel. I don't want to say her name. She's a Jehovah's Witness."

"I don't sleep. I don't eat. I breathe. You know President Obama? He never sleeps. Jesus never sleeps. He just takes a sword. God helps me."

"Would you like an orange?"
He wouldn't take no for an answer and handed me not one, but two.

"MY MOTHER MUST HAVE KNOWN WHAT MY FATHER WAS DOING EVEN BEFORE HE RAPED ME." —REBECCA

"I first got depressed in my 20s. Everything seemed crowded up and dark in my head. I didn't have delusions, but I just felt terrible and like I was always running on empty.

"I got married during those years, but it didn't work out. I was out of whack emotionally. I let him talk me into it because I thought I loved him, but it didn't last.

"I became real depressed again a few times in my 30s and had to be hospitalized. Then I got a heart attack, but I survived it and was still doing okay and still working. But when I was 38, I was in a real bad wreck. One of those big, long trucks hit the back of my car. I flipped underneath the steering wheel and slammed my head. Ever since then I don't think as clearly and can't remember things as well. I have trouble adding and subtracting. I can't figure out the change I owe when I'm in a store, and I get very confused when I'm under even a little stress. I used to be very smart. I had gotten a full scholarship to college when I was 18 and worked as a typist for 22 years.

"The truck accident was a real disaster for me. Not only was my ability to think hurt, but I was never able to forget the moment that the truck hit me. For 10 years, I had nightmares about it when I was asleep and flashbacks when I was awake. Whenever I saw or heard a large truck, I went into a panic. I'm getting better now because I'm taking Prozac, but I still get scared and my heart races when I see a truck.

"When I was in my 40s, I started having problems with an old injury to my leg that had occurred when I had fallen off my bike

at 16. I began to have trouble walking. I had to retire early from my job.

"I didn't expect to be homeless, but my Social Security didn't carry me. I found myself in a mess that I couldn't get out of. I had enough money for rent, but I didn't have enough to pay for the security deposit, so I could never get a room. I tried to save my money by living in a shelter three weeks of the month. I spent the last week on a bus going back and forth to Reno. You could get a very cheap ticket then. I kind of used the bus as a moving shelter.

"I guess I also left during that last week of the month because I needed to run around. I'd get real excited, thinking I was going to save my money for a room, and I'd do a lot of running. I mean, I was actually running, even with my bad leg. I was free, no roof over my head, and no restrictions and rules to follow. It was difficult to sleep during that week, maybe because I was drinking a lot of coffee. It was a wonderful, exhilarating feeling, but I also felt kind of crazy. The doctors told me I had manic depression. That's how I lived for eight years, in and out of shelters and buses.

"Three years ago, I broke my ankle while I was walking off a curb. And a year later I developed cancer of the ovaries. It spread to my lungs and my liver, but I think the radiation treatment they gave me stopped it from spreading further. Then a few months ago, I broke my wrist getting off a bus. That's what this cast on my right arm is all about. So I've had a difficult few years.

"But the good part is that I got into a special psychiatry program at San Francisco General Hospital. The social worker I got, Lisa, has been wonderful. She gave me this stuffed animal when I was going for my radiation. And she's the one who got me this room. The rent is supported by the city. Things have been much more *stable since I moved in here. My nightmares are better, probably because I'm now on Prozac.*

"I'm not depressed anymore, and my anxiety is much better. I've come a long way from where I started.

"I didn't come from the best family. My father died when I was two. I can't remember him exactly, but I was told by my grandmother that he used to carry me around a lot and used to take me to work and everything. He kind of protected me from my mother. After he died, I was at her mercy. She didn't watch us that closely. I got hurt a lot as a kid. When I was three, I crawled over to the floor heater and fell on it. I got third-degree burns. I don't know where my mother was at the time. Maybe she was in the hospital. She went insane about then and had to be committed for a year. She was real depressed. She cried and yelled a lot. I'd be real embarrassed about it. My grandparents took care of us then.

"We tried getting back together as a family later on, but it didn't work out. My mother was still not right in her head, and she married a man who was really abusive. I was six years old. I remember that year because it was the year I broke my arm. My stepfather drank a lot and was real violent. He had guns and things. He was sexually abusive, too. He was real forward and everything to me and my sister. Mostly he just touched me and messed around, but it went on for several years.

"When I was 12, he got real bad. He jumped on me in the middle of the night and tore me open, and I had to be sewn up. We went to court over that. And the judge told me the next time it happened, to get one of those guns and shoot him. But he only got a year in jail. The judge seemed to be on his side even though he could see I couldn't help myself because I had been asleep

when my stepfather came into my room. I blame my mother because she must have known what my father was doing even before he raped me. But I guess it was hard for her because she was so depressed.

"After that, my mother separated from him, but he still had visitation rights when he got out of jail. The strange thing is that I had forgotten about the rape until his death last year. It was always present as a kind of dark memory, but I couldn't recall the details until my sister told me he had died. He got away with a lot in his life.

"I guess the only real parent I had was my father, for my first two years. I don't have a real picture of him in my mind, but I have a sense of him, a kind of warm feeling of someone being there. I use the sensation to comfort myself sometimes. When things get out of hand, when I've had a big day or when I'm in a lot of pain or when the stress builds up, I try to remember that someone was once close by. It's helped me survive."

"I'M GOIN' TO SELL THESE SHOES FOR $10,000."

—THE SHOE SALESMAN

"Let me give you a shoeshine," he said as I passed him on Market Street.

"You got it,' I responded. *"How much do you charge?"*

"One dollar for a shine."

"I can do better than that for you."

"No, I'm just trying to make an honest living. I make $60 a month."

He held up a pair of women's shoes and asked me if I wanted to buy them.

"See these shoes? These are the world's greatest shoes. I'm goin' to sell these shoes for $10,000, and that will get me off the street. I've shined and sold shoes most of my life. I call myself a 'buffeton.'"

"What is that?" I asked.

"Someone who buffs shoes. I'm here three days a week. The other days, I have a second job. I take care of police horses. I'm also a certified public accountant. I live in a church. They let me sleep in an office. My sister pays my rent. Do you like my beard?"

"I like it."

"So do I. It keeps the dogs away."

"I sell shoes to the yoga pimps. Yoga pimps don't pimp women. They pimp yachts."

"What do you mean?"

"Well, it's better than saying 'bubera.' And I don't know what 'bubera' means, but it's not as bad as saying 'yoga pimp.'"

"When black men come, the police come and take their shoes. They sell their shoes, and they think that's the way to make money. That's the law of a physician that makes it seem like he's married. That's the way I make money."

He went on in this vein, polishing and shining my shoes, always talking in an animated manner, stopping his story only to ask me occasionally if I wanted to have a drink of his herb mixture. This, he said, was very healthy but "too tight for him." He told me that he had been hospitalized in psychiatric units many times but is doing fine now. His sister is helping him.

———————————————

My 10-year-old tennis sneakers had never looked better than after his 20-minute shine, for which, and despite my protests, he would take only one dollar. I stayed to chat for an hour, not that I understood much of his conversation. I was enchanted by his warmth and friendliness.

This man seemed to be making out okay at the moment and survived partially because of his spirit, his warmth, his infectious enthusiasm, his great sense of humor, and his enjoyment of hard work. In fact, he seemed to love and take pride in his work far more than most other people on the planet. He was certainly more friendly and outgoing than most. For whatever reasons, his mental illness hadn't sucked him dry. His life was evidence that even in its fairly severe form, mental illness doesn't have to completely sink people, especially if they have family to rely on.

"TOO MANY PEOPLE ARE DEAD HERE."

—WOMAN FROM HONOLULU

I came upon this woman struggling with her possessions down Market Street. She politely but firmly refused my offer of help.

"I came from Honolulu a long time ago. I'm going to move out of San Francisco. Too many people are dead here. Six thousand people suddenly dead. People suddenly dead in Santa Rosa, too. I sleep outside most nights because I don't feel safe inside."

"AFTER MY FIRST KILL, IT GOT TO BE NOTHING."

—WALTER

"There's a cop who works for the San Rafael police department whose job it is to hunt the homeless. He rides around the back roads in the hills and finds those of us who live in camps in the woods. If he finds us, he writes us a ticket and moves us out."

I met Walter at the end of the Blithedale Avenue exit ramp from the highway. I had seen him many times at the same spot, which by some unwritten agreement with his colleagues he seemed to own. He explained to me that when anyone else was there panhandling, it was by his consent.

He wasn't interested in talking with me at first, partially because it was hard for him to talk and work at the same time. Specifically, I was distracting him from making eye contact with the drivers and was interfering with his business. He worked there six hours a day, rain or shine, sometimes making only $15—on a good day $50, but on average $20. When I asked him what it was like to stand in the rain and make only $15, which I calculated was $2.50 an hour and represented the total proceeds from 25,000 cars coming off the ramp during that particular day (or .06 cent per car), he answered philosophically that some days were bound to be good and others bad. *"If I have a bad day, I know there will be a good day sometime soon."*

He ultimately warmed up to me and after 15 minutes led me to a little grove of trees under the highway that he used as a place where he could rest, smoke, and get away from the relentless traffic.

"I had a place in the woods on the hill. Hell, I had it for 10 years. The police finally found me by helicopter one night using an

infrared sensor. They seem to have nothing better to do than hunt the homeless camps. If they come on us, we have one hour to move and then they come back with a whole crew and take all your shit. They're not allowed to take your water, but they take everything else. And if you've set up good and you've been there for a while, there's no way you can move all of your stuff in one hour. I've lost everything I owned in six camps to them: sleeping bags, tents, food, everything. That's a lot of stuff to lose. You have to stay hidden real good. We can't have a fire and we can't use lights except for flashlights, and then we have to keep these real low. It seems like I'm always in hiding. It's like Nam.

"I was in Nam for four years. I was 18 when I was drafted. I was on a patrol boat as the rear gunner. We were a floating target every day we went out. And every day we wondered whether it would be our last. We used a lot of pot and booze to quiet our nerves. After a while I stopped feeling as scared because it got to be routine. The good thing is that we would never be attacked without some warning. You always knew when you were going to be shot at because you could smell the sweet opium that the Cong used. Also, you would see sniper fire from the trees. And then you just turn the machine guns on them and cut them down.

"My first kill, it was hand-to-hand fighting. I had a knife with a long blade, a kind of bayonet. He had one, too. He made a big mistake, and I slit his throat. And then I threw up. After my first kill, it got to be nothing. You become an expert because you train and train and train.

"The only other time I threw up was after I killed a kid. It made me sick. He was only seven years old, but he was armed to the teeth. He had a grenade hidden under his arm. He raised his elbow and let the grenade drop and then ran for the trees. I only had a few

seconds to get rid of the grenade, and then I blew a hole in his chest seven inches wide with my rifle.

"Even though you get used to having your life in danger every day, it was still no joke. You depended on your buddies, but you didn't want to get too close to them. You joked around at night and drank beers and smoked pot and stuff but never got to know them too well. You didn't want to make friends because friends die.

"When I was in the jungle, I was always loaded. I had two ankle guns, two side pistols, an M-16, an M-14, and knives. When I came back from Nam, it was really rough. I had nightmares every single night. Every time a car backfired I hit the ground, thinking it was an incoming explosive. I was ready to kill, but I didn't have anything to do it with. I felt totally naked. The PTSD program at the VA hospital really helped me. Going through my story over and over again finally took away the nightmares, but it took years.

"I started drinking before I went to Nam. Every weekend was a party in my parents' house. Both of them drank, and my sister was an alcoholic. After I went to Nam, I began to drink more heavily, and when I returned to the States, I drank even more to quiet my nerves, help me sleep, and take away the nightmares. I was a heavy drinker for 30 years. Two years ago, I found out that I had hepatitis C. It hit me that my life was really on the line. I stopped drinking cold turkey.

"You won't see me here much anymore because I saved up enough to rent a trailer. It will be the first time I've been inside since I came back from Nam."

"I SLEEP WHERE THE FROG PEOPLE LIVE." —RHONDA

Rhonda was sitting on a box outside a restaurant, talking to herself and trying to keep warm with her jacket and the extra pair of pants someone had given her. She had been sleeping on the street for months, although she had been given a room when she was last discharged from the psychiatric unit. *"I just didn't want to stay in that room."* Her parents and seven brothers and sisters live a few miles away. They bring her food three times a month but don't want to take her in. *"I don't know why they don't want me."*

When I initially approached her, she was shy, diffident, hesitant, and almost inaudible, but when I asked about her family, her whole personality changed.

"My family came from Puerto Rico, Norway, Jerusalem, some-where else. We were once rich, but some people followed us home and then played all kinds of goddamn sorts of tricks on us and took everything we had. They gave us a lot of bullshit, a lot of junk and goddamn trash, and stole every goddamn thing we looked at.

"My family didn't come from goddamn anywhere and didn't have goddamn nothing when we arrived. We had no goddamn body else. We had no goddamn mother or father.

"I sleep where the frog people live—on the beaches. They combine with real frogs. Seafood, that's what I mean, heliomonsters and all of that, hamburger monsters. They kill you for hamburgers."

THE GANG: MAX, SABRINA, AND JED

I came upon Max, Sabrina, and Jed one raw fall morning in Golden Gate Park. They were huddled together, shivering, trying to warm themselves by passing around a bottle of some greenish alcoholic mix. As a group, they were a bit intimidating to approach, but summoning my courage, I commented to them on how cold it was, and they affably reached back to me. By the end of a day of hanging out with them, I had more or less been included in their little gang. However, as the afternoon sun dropped behind the trees, and San Francisco's cold fog began blowing in, I became increasingly self-conscious about the warm home and real dinner I would return to that evening. They would spend that night and the next night, and the next, shivering in doorways. Unaccountably, they didn't seem to begrudge me my life of privilege, revealing much more generosity than I would have been able to muster had I been in their shoes.

"I'M NOT PROUD OF SOME OF THE SHIT I DID." —MAX

Max was a loud, foul-mouthed, funny alpha male who dominated the whole scene, deciding where they sat, what they drank, when they came, and when they went. No one else spoke when he was carrying forth. Everything was for show: his stories, his tattoos, his antics. What was true and what wasn't? Who could tell?

"I spent 14 years in the marines. I was a corpsman in Vietnam. My great-granddaddy was in the Civil War, and my daddy was head of cardiology in the navy. I lost both of my sons in Iraq. So I feel totally fucked.

"You wanna hear something? This broke my goddamn heart. When I was in Nam, a guy named Joe Eliot came back from patrol.

He had 13 days left on his tour of duty. I don't know what the fuck happened. He sat right next to me. He pulled out his gun, put it to his head, and blew his brains out. They say that the last couple of weeks of duty, people are vulnerable. The last few days, that's either when you get blown up or take your own life.

"Well, I'll tell you something. I killed people in Nam. Someone fucked me over when I was in prison. I had gasoline smuggled in and set him on fire. I'm not proud of that! I fuckin' despise violence now.

"I had this crazy Native American Indian buddy who wrapped a cloth around an arrow, stuck it in some Crisco®, lit it, and shot it a mile. I swear to God! He stood out on the patio, pulled that bow back 65 pounds. 'Don't do it. Don't fuckin' do it, man!' I said. He knew exactly what he was going to do. He said, 'Watch this!' Famous last words, right? 'Trust me on this one,' he said. That goddamn fucker went 1,000 meters as the crow flies! It looked like a comet, man. Within two minutes, we heard sirens. That motherfucker! The arrow had landed on someone's roof and set the house on fire. 'You crazy-assed Indian!' I said."

"NOW I'M HERE, AND I'M NOT QUITE SURE WHERE I'M GOING." —SABRINA

Sabrina was a sweet, gentle, quiet woman who sat shaking, with a blanket wrapped around her. Occasionally, she'd break out laughing at Max's jokes. At other times, she'd become tearful.

"I'm new at this homeless thing. I just got here on Saturday— from Lincoln, California. Twenty-six dollars was what I had, and it just about paid for a one-way ticket here, so I got on the bus and came. Now I'm here, and I'm not quite sure where I'm going.

"I was living with my boyfriend in Lincoln. He was my best friend for 15 years before we started living together. But then things went bad. He was taking speed and slamming me around a bit. We broke up. Then we got back together. We went back and forth, back and forth. Two months ago, I spent a week cleaning him up, and right away he starting tweaking. I hadn't been drinking for 31 days, but as soon as I found out he was using, I began drinking again.

"I started going downhill fast, so I went to a Christian alcohol rehab facility. As soon as I got out, I called my boyfriend and found that he was living with my closest girlfriend. So I lost my lover and my girlfriend, the two closest people to me. I felt completely betrayed. A friend took me in, but I started stealing from her liquor cabinet. I got a little money and came to San Francisco. And I guess I'm here trying to numb myself.

"I come from a long line of alcoholics. I've drunk all my life, even though I had two jobs and went to college at the same time. I was three weeks away from getting my bachelor's. I did all that while I was raising three kids. It's all gone now.

"I'm not close to my parents. I don't know who my real dad is, but my stepdad molested me for two years, starting when I was 13. My stepdad and mom are still together even though I eventually told my mother what he did. I didn't tell her at the time because I felt too guilty. I blamed myself. It doesn't matter how right or wrong it is, when someone's touching you like that, you have certain reactions. It felt good. He came in the night, and I pretended I was asleep.

"I hated my mom. She was a prude about sex and once told me she didn't even like it. I blamed her for my dad coming in, 'cause I thought if she had sex with my stepdad, he would have left me alone. I also hated her because she should've known. How do you not know something like that? It was her responsibility to know, and you know, protect your kids.

"Some people say that when a father or stepfather does that kind of thing, it makes it impossible for a girl to like sex, but it didn't seem to have that effect on me. I became promiscuous as a teenager and liked it. As soon as I graduated from high school, I left, and I got pregnant.

"I've been up all night and I'm freezing. It might also be a bit of the DTs."

"I CAME TO SAN FRANCISCO TO DIE." —JED

Jed didn't say a word for the first two hours I spent with him and the gang, but once drawn out, he was exceedingly reflective.

"Once you've been in prison, it's like a life sentence because it follows you for the rest of your days. I haven't been convicted of a crime in nine years, but I still can't get a job. I'm tired and down, and there's not much I can do about it. Prozac helped level me out for a while, but then it stopped working. I do stupid shit out here. I know better. I just get drunk and don't care.

"Some guys have the mountains in their blood. They come down to a city, but they always go back to the mountains. For me, it's the streets. Out here, nothing matters. I came to San Francisco to die. My only hope is that I'll die drunk and never feel any pain."

"SOMEONE BROKE INTO MY HOTEL ROOM AND STOLE MY EYE." —ROSE

"My mother never liked me. When I was 12, the guy she was living with began molesting me. I didn't tell her because I knew she wouldn't do a damn thing. The whole neighborhood knew what was going on.

"A year later, I got pregnant and had a son by some other guy. I didn't know how to protect myself because my mother never taught me. When I was 14 I began jumping out of my bedroom window and seeing George, who was 30 years older than me. When my mom found out, she threw all my clothes on the street, gave me $5, and told me to leave. I moved in with George and ended up becoming the mother of three boys and three girls.

"I left George because he used to beat me up so bad. Once he stabbed me in the neck. After I moved out, he snuck into my house one night and tried to kill me on account of him being jealous. He shot at me four times with a revolver. One bullet hit my forehead. I had our baby in my arms and our little girl next to me. If I hadn't leaned back, he would have killed his own baby.

"When I got older, I got into the drug life in a big way. See these needle marks? Then I began doing crack and turning tricks to pay for it. It's lucky I don't have AIDS. If I met a guy and his wife was sick or something and he just wanted to do his little thing, and go about his business, and if he treated me all right, then fine. I'd do it with him, and that's it. But if he tried to misuse me, I'd set his ass on fire.

"I was homeless off and on for years. I'd sleep in doorways and sometimes in cardboard boxes. I know what it's like to be cold. It's why I give homeless people my blankets and my clothes.

"I used to read a lot. But a few years ago, my right eye got infected and the doctor had to take it out. I've been wearing a prosthesis since then. Once I had it sitting in a glass of water beside my bed. Someone broke into my hotel room and stole it. Can you believe it? Stole my own eye from my own room!

"Women who had love as children are happy. Sometimes I watch them in front of the hotel, laughing and joking and having a good time. I can't join in because I don't fit. I never had nobody

to cry to, nobody to talk to. I never had a girlfriend. I don't know what it is about me, what it is I do wrong. Must be something. I'm lonely all the time. Sometimes I try to buy friendship with crack, sometimes with sex. I keep putting myself out there and getting hurt. Even someone bad is better than being alone.

"I'm scared to do drugs by myself because I'm afraid I might try to kill myself. I know that I'd be taking the easy way out, but I lay up two or three days in my room, and just want out. I want to go through that door, but I'm scared to do it. Every time I'm at the subway station, and the train is comin' down the track, I feel like that train is calling me to jump. And I have to physically grab hold of something to stop myself. Drugs become your comfort, your friend, a bad friend. They're supposed to make you forget, but I don't forget. I still be empty inside. I just go 'round the corner and cry to myself. I know time is not long for me.

"I so much want a puppy that I could I talk to, that I can love. I'd feed him before I fed myself. It would fill up my heart. I'm afraid to volunteer at a pet place because I'd be afraid either that I'd kidnap some dog or that I'd fall in love with it and then I'd lose it."

"IT'S HARD HAVING A RELATIONSHIP WHEN YOU'RE LIVING ON THE STREET." —DONNA

"I've been homeless for 13 years, since I lost my job as a maid in a hotel. I've lived in the same spot outside for 10 years. I'm eligible for GA [General Assistance], but I can't get it because I have a bail warrant out for my arrest and if I went into the welfare office, I'd get picked up and put in jail. My original offense was possession of crack, and I got out on bail. I didn't go back to court because I was afraid I'd be convicted and have to go to jail. I haven't been in jail that much, about five times in my whole life, but I hate it.

"If I had the money, I'd live in an SRO [single-room-occupancy hotel]—if it didn't have roaches or rats. But those places are often terrible. When my boyfriend and I first got to San Francisco and started living in a room, I'd have to stay up all night long, sitting on the window sill with a fishing pole and poke the rats out of the bed so my boyfriend could get a good night's sleep and get up for work the next morning. It's not that there were so many rats, but one, in my opinion, is too many. They don't bother me as long as I see them coming, you know. When they run up on you, that's when it's bad.

"I wash my hands a thousand times a day, but they still get dirty digging in the garbage. It's easy to get sick when you live on the streets. I just got out of the hospital yesterday for pneumonia and a hernia.

"But I find all kinds of things in the garbage. I found these shoes that I'm wearing. Once, years ago, I was looking in a garbage can for a tissue to blow my nose, and I found this leather purse with a $10, $20, and a $100 bill in it. Another time I found a wallet with a credit card. It was a corporate credit card, unlimited. We got

sleeping bags, iPods, everything. Being the honest citizen that I am, I put the wallet in the mailbox.

"If I had kept all the blankets, sleeping bags, and backpacks I've found over the years, I could open my own sports shop. But it's all been stolen. Homeless people steal from homeless people. If you turn your back for one second, your things are gone. Blankets are especially tough, because they're too heavy to lug around all day and you're forced to stash them someplace. When you come back to get them at night, sometimes they're there and sometimes they're not. Today I was sleeping over on that bench, and someone stole my cigarettes, my food, and my lighter. And they were right beside me!

"It's hard having a relationship when you're living on the street. My boyfriend always wants his way. I tell him he's got an attitude. But he's adorable—strawberry blond and built like a brick shithouse. He's 44, 10 years younger than me. We both smoke crack, which makes us irritable, and we have different hustles, you know. He likes to go on binges and be up for three or four days, but I can't really do that. When he's been awake for too long, he gets mad at everything. Crack is the only thing I do, but he mixes it with other drugs. Another problem is that he's been in jail over and over again for theft, and he's also violated his parole in Delaware, so he's always worried that he'll be picked up.

"Also, he's not a morning person. This morning, he got grouchy because the department of public works sprayed the sidewalk and wet my half of the blanket. I wanted to share his half, which made him irritable. The last person I had a relationship with wasn't a morning person either. He broke four of my ribs with his fist over a disagreement we had about a taco one morning. We're *still best friends. I should have known better than to argue with him in the morning.*

"Living on the streets is not so bad. I'm a survivor. My mother left me right after I was born, and I guess I'm doing all right. I love to read. That's mostly what I do. In five years, I'll probably be doing the same thing: just reading and tryin' to make it."

"THE DEVIL IS HERE!" —MARIA

I was walking down Mission Street and came upon a woman struggling to get into her house with a key. I asked if I could help, at which moment her mother opened the door, discovered that I was a psychiatrist, and with an insistency that could not easily be resisted, invited me into their house.

The daughter had been hospitalized in the psychiatric ward at the city hospital several times, and was taking medication that had been prescribed for her at a public outpatient clinic.

The father had died the previous year, and mother and daughter were struggling to make ends meet, keep up the house, and pay their medical bills. The daughter repeatedly expressed her fear that the hospital would refuse to treat her if she couldn't pay her bills.

Speaking mostly in Spanish, and constantly talking over each other, the two women took me by the hand from room to room, and with warm hospitality and enormous pride, showed me each one of their hundreds of religious objects and paintings. At various points, the daughter talked about the Devil.

"The Devil is here! I don't want to know anything about the Devil. I hear voices, but I don't bother with them. I have the head and beard of Christ right in my room. The Devil came into the house because my sister brought in bad underwear. God took away everything. Something happened, but I don't know what. Jesus keeps the Devil small."

"WHENEVER I LIVE INSIDE, I START THINKING ABOUT WHAT I'VE LOST." —JONATHAN

I met this man on Howard Street lugging a cart behind him. He had alcohol on his breath, and he had a blank look on his face until he began talking about what had happened in his life.

"I was married for 15 years. I had two children. I worked as a mechanic. Things were good. About 20 years ago, I found my wife sleeping with my best friend. I got depressed, started drinking, and couldn't stop. I lost my job and began living on the streets. I've never been able to go back.

"Whenever I live inside, I start thinking about what I've lost. When I live outside, I have to keep thinking about where I'm going to get my next meal, where I'm going to sleep, who's trying to steal from me. I don't have time to think about the mess I've made of my life."

MAN WITH A CANE —JESSIE

I met Jessie in his tiny, musty hotel room, where he had lived for many years. He had a serious organic brain disorder, probably a result of his heavy drinking and head injuries from alcohol-related falls. Despite the fact that the alcohol was slowly killing him, and he was hanging onto life by a slender thread, he continued to drink, and at the time I met him, he had tripped in the street and broken his arm and leg. He managed to survive for some time with the help of his social worker, a meals-on-wheels program, and other supportive services.

Eventually, one December, he was admitted to the public hospital in San Francisco. Through the tenacious efforts of the hospital social worker, his son and daughter were located in Texas. He was moved to a nursing home near them. Without alcohol and in a more structured living situation, he is reportedly doing better than at any time in the past 10 years.

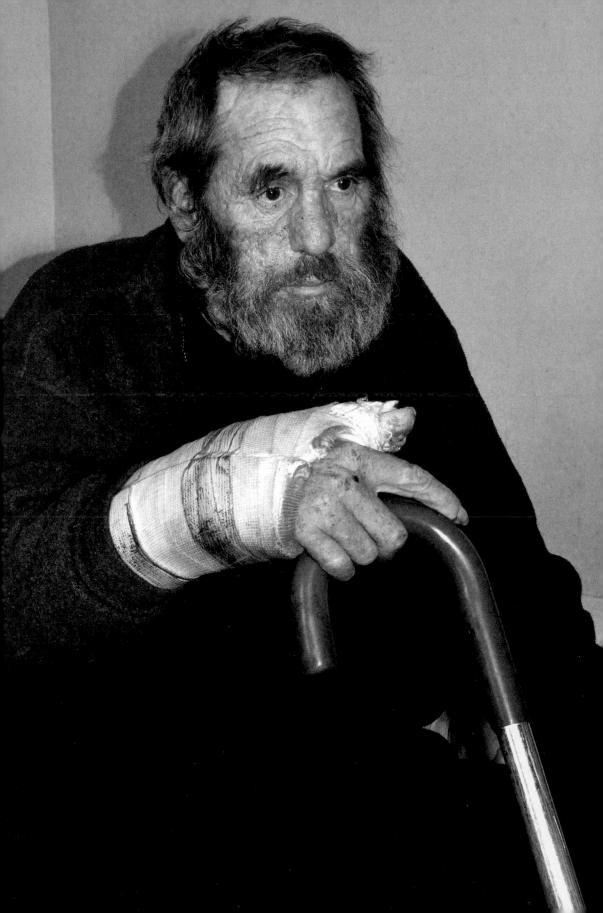

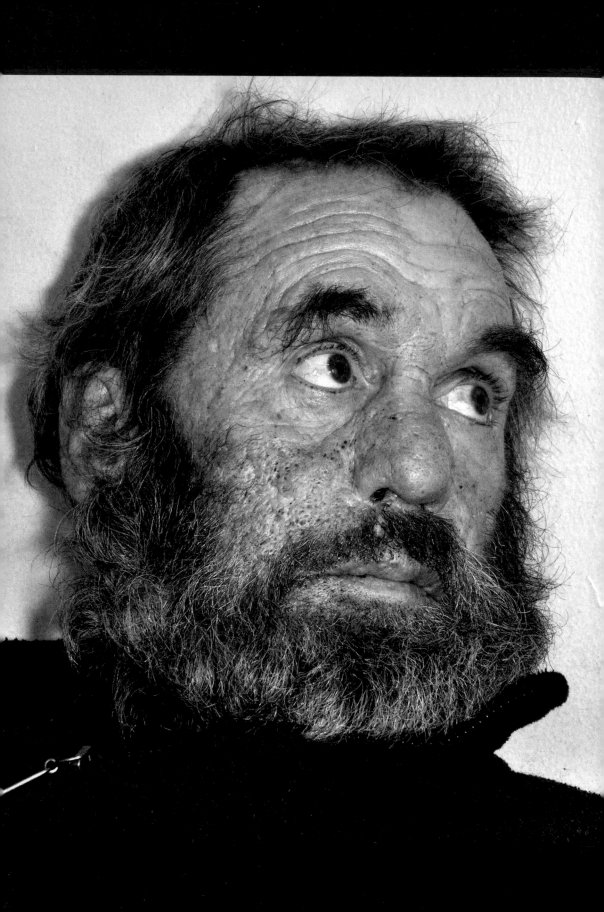

"MY MAMA TRADED MY BICYCLE FOR A SIX-PACK OF BOOZE." —LEE

"I came from Louisiana. My mama and daddy had a lot of mouth when they were drunk. One night when I was only a kid, she found him at a bar, pulled him outside, and tried to run him down with her car. Another night he came home drunk and my three sisters and me, we were so scared that we hid in the bathroom until he went to sleep.

"One Christmas when I was seven, we all got bicycles from the welfare department. A few days later, we come home from school and couldn't find 'em. 'Mama, where are our bikes?' 'Oh, I don't know,' she said. I learned later that she had traded my bicycle for a six-pack of booze.

"One afternoon, she and her sister got drunk and started fightin'. My mama hauled off and broke her sister's jaw. She needed pins to keep her jaw together for three months.

"The neighbors would see us walkin' down the road and would yell at us, 'Well, your mama is nothin' but a bootleggin' whore. She got every man in the house drinkin' and doing it with her.' I couldn't defend myself or her or what went on in the house 'cause I had such a bad stutterin' problem that nobody 'cept one of my sisters could understand me. I felt helpless, like I was in an empty, dark room, in a dark spot, dark ring line. My mama didn't have patience with my stuttering. And my daddy would just laugh at me. I carried that with me all my life.

"We used to go 'round the neighborhood beggin' for food 'cause we was always hungry. It was hard to concentrate on books when all we could think about was our stomachs. Sometimes we got

lucky and the teachers gave us food. When we'd asked my mama for food, she'd tell us to look in the 'frigerator. When we told her there was none, she'd say, 'Go over to your auntie's house and ask her.' But our auntie didn't have any more food than we did, because she was always drunk, same as my mama.

"When I was 11, the school called the welfare department about us. A woman came out to our house, but she didn't come back for a year. Finally, we were put in foster care. My foster mom wanted to adopt me because of the money she'd get paid. My foster daddy wanted to adopt me because they had no boys, and he wanted a son. So he's looking out on that. So I got lucky. I got a family.

"Once when I went back to visit my mama, I found her locked in the bathroom, tryin' to drink herself to death. They took her to the hospital. The doctors wanted to give her medicine. I told 'em, 'She has a drinkin' problem and a drawback problem—drawing back from her family. You can dope her up with medicine all you like and it ain't goin' to change nothin'. Because she has a gene for the disease, and your medicine ain't going to do nothin' for that gene.' Drawback is like a door shuttin' in your face. Like a wall that puts you in a hole and shuts the door on you, shuts it on you. You see, when you have a drawback, you don't want to do anything. You don't want to cook, you don't want to associate, all you want to do is sit in your room and cry. My sister had the gene, too, because she has a drawback problem. Her husband would go into her room and say to her, 'Judy, we is all hungry.' She don't look up, she don't answer, so he'd go to the Chinese restaurant and bring back some food. When he married her, he didn't know she had it, didn't know nothin' about her. 'Well, now you know!' I tell him.

"I've lived in different places, and now I'm here, livin' on the streets, luggin' this cart around with me. The rubber is comin' off *its wheels, but I put duct tape around it. I spend a lot of time at Bible studies at church and that's where I get a lot of my food. But flashbacks of things I blocked as a child come back on me. I can't seem to get away from 'em. You don't miss nothin' as a child."*

"LIFE ON THE STREETS ISN'T EASY, BUT IT'S NOT DESPERATELY HARD."

I came across this woman talking to herself and doing a cross-word puzzle.

"Life on the streets isn't easy, but it's not desperately hard. I'm sleeping on the streets and eating out of garbage cans. I have two or three spots that I sleep, but I don't want to say where. I tried to get on SSI, but I couldn't get on the list, or whatever. That's all I want to talk about."

"THE PSYCH MEDS MADE ME ITCH SO BAD I COULDN'T STOP SCRATCHING MYSELF."

I met this woman at a fast-food restaurant. She didn't want to talk except to tell me she had been hospitalized in a psychiatric ward and had been given meds that made her itch so badly that she couldn't stop scratching her face.

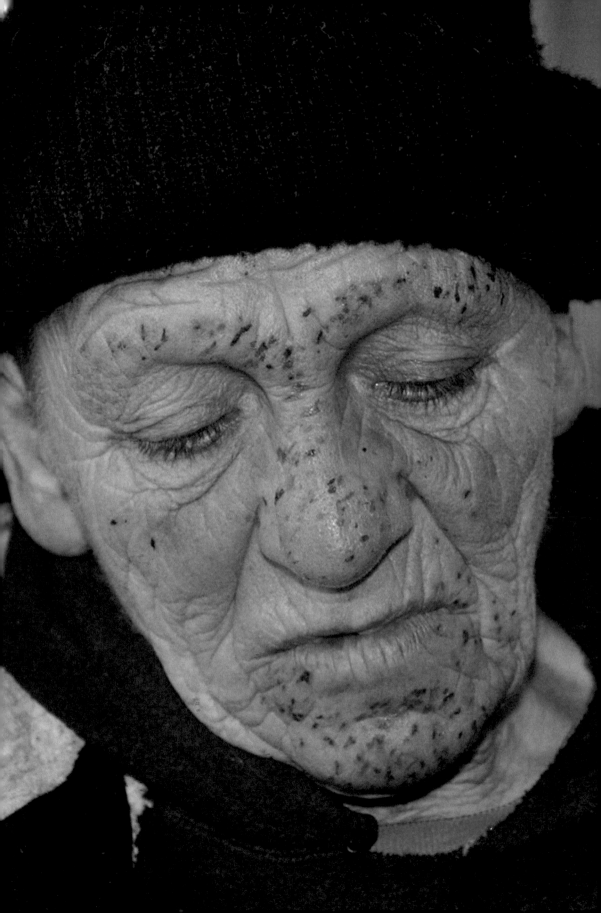

"EVERYONE SAYS HOW TOUGH IT IS TO BE HOMELESS, BUT I'M GOOD AT IT." —VINCE

"I lived at the Mission Hotel for five years. What you get for almost your whole welfare check is a tiny room with a public bathroom. I liked the other residents, but I couldn't take the lice, the roaches, the bedbugs, the mice. I always had the feeling I was being eaten alive. One night a bedbug had a feast on my blood. He could hardly walk he was so full and fat. He had made a total pig of himself. The hotel disinfected the room, but after that, I was so afraid of being infected again by someone who might be bringing bedbugs into my room, I wouldn't let anyone sit on my bed.

"My woman, Linda, wouldn't stay there with me after the bedbugs bit her. She wasn't goin' for that. Also, it seemed like every time she came over, the mice wanted to come out and play. Also, the roaches would always be munching on things when she was there. She'd wake up and say, 'Take me home!'

"The Mission is the largest welfare hotel in the city. It has more than 300 people. About 50 percent of the people are mentally ill. If you add the drug addicts, it's much more. Most of the people, they're very low-functioning. Some have been there for years. Basically, they can't afford anything else or they have no place else to go. Or they stay because they've gotten used to it and feel safe there.

"Many of the people stay in their rooms and don't say much to anyone. One day I started talking to a guy who always kept to himself. People took advantage of him, took his crack. He didn't even know how much money he was supposed to get from his case manager. Sometimes I got high with him. And he took a liking to me. When I was getting ready to leave the hotel and told

him, I saw his eyes getting wet. I asked him, 'Don, you all right?' He said to me, 'You're my only friend.'

"I met up with Linda in 2001. I had been seeing girls only for sex, but this one girl, I kinda liked, and she kinda stuck around a while. I couldn't get rid of her. So we hooked up. When I couldn't stand the Mission anymore, I went to live with her, but it was difficult. She wanted me to live her way—in her apartment, spending the whole day in front of the TV, drinking beer and smoking. She kept pressuring me and trying to control me. I began getting depressed and started losing interest in her. When I started spending more time on my own, she started denying me sex. Then I really lost interest. We men, we very simple, very easy to placate. Fuck us, feed us, don't mess with our minds, and we cool. We can last a long time on that diet. One day I upped and left and have been living on the streets since then.

"Being on the streets is the thing that helps me with my depression. It's the only place I don't have any obligations to anyone. All I got to do on the streets is take care of myself. I can get high when I want, drunk when I want, talk to whoever I want. It's all for me. No one expects me to give them anything. It's the only way I can keep what I have. When I'm anywhere else, people always want something from me.

"Everyone says how tough it is to be homeless, but I've done this before. I'm good at it. I'm used to it. I know how to survive it. Since I've been outside, I lost 30 pounds, my diabetes and hypertension are under control, I'm stronger, and even my arthritis is better. Being on the streets is good for my health. Crazy, ain't it?

"Sometimes I sleep in a shelter, in a chair all night, because there's usually no empty beds. I do it for two to three days max, and then *if I can't get into a bed after that, I get me some ground cover like a cardboard box and find me a cubbyhole, and sleep there. Otherwise, I get on the subway and ride for five or six hours. Even though I'm sitting up, I can sleep because the rail sound is soothing. One night I was on the train for seven hours, back and forth, back and forth.*

"People who have to use the bathroom on the subway, they outta luck. They closed all the subway bathrooms since 911. So people have to pee where they can. I was on the subway once, I peed on the station wall. There was nowhere else to do it. What was I going to do?

"The reason I was late meeting you today is that I had to change my clothes. I was in the subway, and I just couldn't hold it anymore. I was running up the escalator to go to the public bathroom outside, and I started peeing in my pants. It was humiliating.

"San Francisco can get cold. Even though other places like San Diego is warmer, the police there are tougher, not very tolerant of the homeless. They ran them all out. Even in San Francisco, in Mayor Frank Jordan's time, they tried to outlaw homelessness, tried to ship us all out. Made it illegal to be homeless. Can you believe that? If it's illegal to be homeless, give 'em a home. You homeless, you go to jail. That's your new home. Crazy laws. Frank Jordan was a nut.

"The city's new policy of Care Not Cash started out with a big bang because the city had empty rooms to give people in exchange for their welfare checks. Now the rooms are drying up, so people have to give their money to the city, $360 of the $425, just to live in a shelter, on a cot for nine months until a room opens up. The same people who used to be staying in the shelter for free now have to pay for it. They don't want that.

"And shelters are not much better than the streets. The staff who work in the shelters have no real training. They're just doing a low-paying job. The people who need a bed in a shelter have sunk really low in their lives. In order to help them turn their lives around, you have to be able to touch them, and in order to touch them, you have to have some kind of training to recognize when they're hurting. A lot of these people, when they're hurting, automatically go into their 'big bad motherfucker' mode. But the staff don't seem to understand it. All they can see is their attitude, and they say, 'Well, you gotta get outta here. You can't bring that attitude in here.' This 'fuck you' attitude is just hurt, plain and simple. And a lot of the people who use that attitude actually prefer that you get tough with them, because that's what they're used to, that's what they're expecting, that's what they know how to deal with. 'Throw me out, I don't give a fuck!'

"The so-called 'support hotels,' the hotels with social workers, are even worse than the shelters in some ways, because the social workers at least have some training and ought to know better. But they don't do anything. I always wonder why they ain't helping the clients. They see someone needs shoes, why they ain't bringing them to Salvation Army to get shoes? They see people who are reclusive, why they ain't saying, 'Hey, let's get some coffee together'? It's the social worker gotta make the move. You can't expect the client to do it. If the client could, he wouldn't be there in the first place.

"Once I made $10 selling my blood for a diabetes study at the hospital. I used it to by drugs, but the two guys who sold them to me gave me bad stuff. I came back and they were still standing there, like 'Fuck you! We're not afraid of you!' I stabbed one of them in the side and cut off the other one's pinky finger. Another time, I bit a guy's cheek off because he tried to rob me, and I didn't *even have any money. I always carry this—a jawbreaker, golf ball in a sock. Hit someone under the chin will break a jaw. My mama would be proud if she were alive.*

"She passed away in '92. Been gone a while. I miss her. She was my best friend. She was a bitty thing, 5'2". But she was real tough, mean also. My father was tall, 6'4". When I was a kid, I heard them arguing one day. I came runnin' down the stairs to help my mama, just in time to see my stepfather going through the plate-glass window and then over the hedge, drapes and all. That's what saved him—the drapes wrapped around him. It was my dad I needed to help, not my mama.

"One time she shot him. He had other kids before they were married. His oldest daughter come over one day and got to arguing with my mama. My mama pulled out a pistol and shot at her twice. My daddy jumped in front of her, and he took two bullets in the chest. Now you know what kinda mean she was. He was a big man, but he had to go to the hospital.

"Funny, she wasn't mean to me. I was her favorite. I was the good son. I was a straight-A student. I never gave her any problems at all. I was student body president, athlete, on the chess club, all that. I had a job after school, I cut lawns, I made me a little money. I didn't become a problem until I was 30. And then I started getting a little wild. I never got arrested, though, until I was 32. But I've been arrested three times in the last year, selling drugs, selling crack. I was picked up by an undercover cop. I was in jail for 20 days, was let out, and was back two hours later for selling again.

"People say, 'Well, why do people around here sell drugs? Why don't they work?' But selling is their work, and it's good work. The amount of money you can make in a low-end job like McDonald's

is trivial compared to what you can make selling drugs. There are very smart people around here who maybe graduated high school, maybe didn't. But they don't have a skill and can't get a reasonable paying job. In the 'hood, people have no respect for someone who's working at a low-paid job. People get on your case, you're working at McDonald's. It means you don't have any balls, no initiative. Young people in some dead-end job working under a boss eight hours a day see other people working for themselves selling drugs three hours a day, and they say, 'That could be me.' And then they start working the street. But then the street takes them and keeps them.

"But you get jailed even for possession in this state. It's ridiculous. People who are using are just victimizing themselves. It would be like putting someone in jail for not taking his insulin. It costs the government unbelievable amounts of wasted money.

"At one time, they used to call crack 'nigger rocks' 'cause it was so cheap that it was the only form of cocaine that blacks could afford. Asians, whites, they ignored it, they didn't use crack. Now you see even white guys walking down the street buying. It's easy to tell because they have the same look—a slow walk, they're lookin' at everybody, they have a big jacket. They're selling. And nobody has a territory here. Anybody can sell. It's a free-for-all. It's free ball.

"Crack has destroyed the black population, set it against itself, brought it down. Crack is one drug that kinda hypnotizes you when you first use it. It feels so good and it's so highly addictive that all you want to do is keep getting high in your room. A crack high comes and goes in 30 seconds, and then you immediately get a longing for more. You get trapped. You're finished. A lot of men don't even want to be bothered with sex anymore. Women, on the other hand, seem to have better sex on crack. That's one reason why women who use crack tend to lose their morals. They're called toss-ups—women who give sexual favors for crack. Often only for $5—a 'nickel.' So they get two things: crack and good sex.

"I don't think people are ever goin' to stop using and selling if they don't have a better option. Now their only option is jail. Now people say, 'I'd rather use and take the chance on goin' to jail.' Jail, losing their so-called freedom, is nothing to a lot of these people. No big deal, because their freedom ain't worth much of anything. It doesn't really give them anything. They're unemployed and not goin' anyplace in life. They're marking time. And many don't expect to live very long. For some of them, jail is actually a relief for a while. They get a roof over their heads, food. They can clean up, and get their health back if they been strung out. Jail lets them live a while longer, go back on the streets, and because they have no place else to go, and nothing else to do, they start using again within hours. It's depressing. Everywhere they go, everybody they know is using. It's their life, it's their friends, it's what they know how to do.

"If the city really wanted to do something to help them, it's gotta do something other than put 'em back on the street, give 'em a welfare check, and expect them to use it to pay for a shitty, overpriced, depressing little room. People would rather live on the streets, smoke crack, and take their chances on getting arrested again. You gotta give 'em something they view as too valuable to lose if they get caught again, like real housing.

"I was the only black working for Bechtel once. I was a draftsman, working on a board. They hired me because they didn't have nobody else at the time, even though I hadn't gone to school for drafting. They had to hire a black. The first job they gave me was designing toilets. When they realized I was good, they gave me *a top job, but nobody talked to me after work or during lunch. They'd go for a drink after work, and didn't invite me. They had a bowling league. They didn't ask me to be on it. I felt lonely and hurt and cut out. I got mad, missed work a couple of times, and they put me on probation. But another guy was missing work, they didn't put him on probation. They gave me the hardest jobs at the worst salary, and that's when I snapped. I asked them, 'How come I'm not invited to the bowling league, how come I have to eat lunch all by myself, how come nobody talks to me, how come I always get the hard jobs? I been here three years. Why do you have me training a guy who just came out of college and he's already making more money than me? He's being paid $2,400 a month. I'm getting paid $600 a month. Why?' They had an award ceremony one year and gave a guy a free three-day trip to Las Vegas for being the top salesman. And I said, 'I'm going to win that next year.' Next year, I made $3 million for the company. Did I get a trip? No fucking way. I got a plaque. Come on!*

"You doin' a good project. Just get out there and talk to people. Some people may want money, they poor, they're out there hustling, but some will talk to you even for no money. Many are lonely and just want to talk to someone. Some want to talk because they feel invisible. It's like, 'I'm here.'"

Two months later, Vince left a message on my answering machine telling me that he was going to the hospital to get detoxed from drugs. He'd been having more problems on drugs than he'd been acknowledging to himself or me.

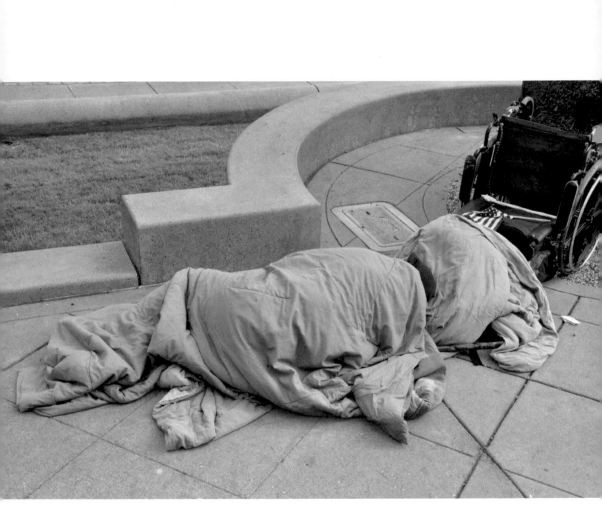

"I WAS LIKE A WOLF. I'D ONLY COME OUT AT NIGHT."

—DON

"I'm the assistant manager of a soup kitchen now, but I'll never, ever forget what kind of life I came from. For over 10 years, I was a drunken bum, living in a campsite along the railroad tracks. Usually, I'd beg for food or eat out of dumpsters. Other times, I'd scrounge for bottles and cans and sell them for 5 cents each to a recycling center. I was like a wolf. I'd only come out at night. I was a recluse. I had a tent, a sleeping bag, and some clothes.

"Before I became a drunk I was happily married, had kids, and earned a good living. But then my wife developed stomach cancer and died. I didn't want to live after that. I was a mess—depressed, crying all the time. Life was a prison of loneliness and missing her. A few months later I began drinking, went through all my money. My wife's treatment had taken most of my money, and alcohol polished the rest off. One night I sat down on a street corner and realized, 'You've got nowhere to go. Man, you're homeless.' I camped under a bridge that night. In the beginning, I was scared stiff I'd be killed. You know, I had read articles in the newspaper about homeless alcoholics being murdered.

"My life was a mess for years until someone told me about this kitchen. When I first came here, I felt as small as a crumb. But the people here took me in without ever putting me down, and slowly I was able to stop drinking, began volunteering here, and reconnected with my family. Four years ago, I became a paid staff member, and a little while later, I was made assistant manager.

"I'd be dead if it weren't for this place."

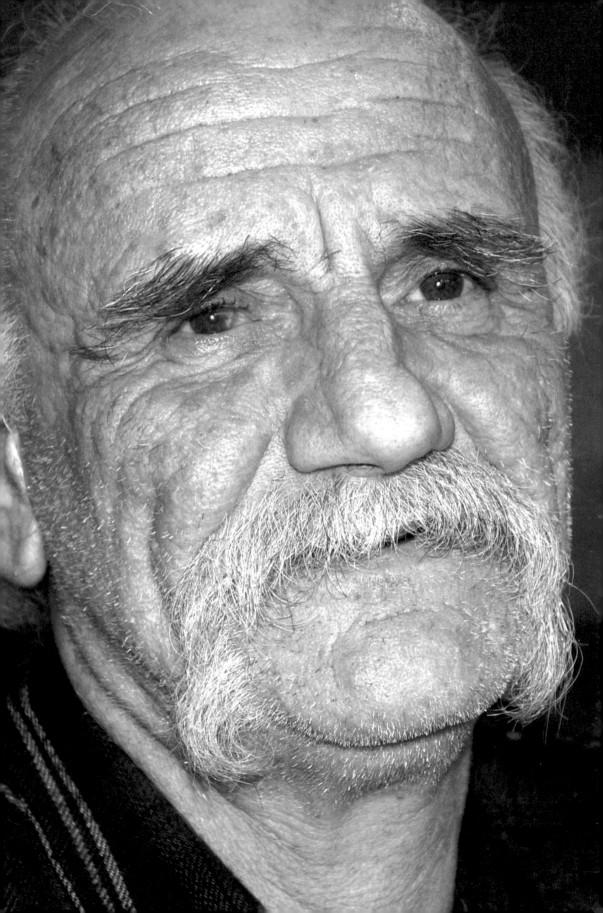

"SOME DAYS, I WAKE UP NOT KNOWING WHO I AM."

—George

"I've had multiple sclerosis since I was 10. I have had some very dramatic episodes. My body has shut down to the point where I can't breathe and I can't swallow. It is terrifying. If it gets too warm, my temperature will go up, like a lizard's. I've been in the hospital the better part of the last two years. They stuck a pacemaker in me.

"They had me on steroids, which was supposed to help my multiple sclerosis, but the steroids gave me osteoporosis, which fractured my hip, and I've been stuck in a wheelchair since then.

"The disease takes away my memory sometimes. Some days, I wake up not knowing who I am. I'm a different character from day to day.

"I've lived a very interrupted life. I'm the only one who's lasted this long with such a bad case of this disease. The most common way that people die with multiple sclerosis is by suicide. They just can't stand the ups and downs, never knowing what part of their bodies are going to go next.

"For a long time, I was a very dangerous person physically. I was what they call a penetration and negotiation specialist for the government. I talked to the Irish Republican Army. I helped make the deal that shut it down. And in return, the government cut me a whole lot of slack when I was caught not having paid $3 million in taxes.

"We burned money as part of the protests against the Vietnam War. Money is nothing. It's no good. It's just paper. We shut down Washington, DC, in 1967. We stopped all the traffic so no one could go to work. I once got sentenced, but the government let me go. I knew too much."

He strummed his guitar for a few minutes and then told me he wanted to go outside for a smoke.

"I WON'T TOUCH THE DEAD BRANCHES OF YOUR FILTH."

—KLAUSS

I met this man in the park near the Ferry Building. He was sitting on a bench talking to himself with an angry intensity. When I approached him, he said, *"You're a murderer in my park and you will be prosecuted in my park. I'm telling you I don't want to hear your shit. And also Herpes, dead lobby ways. I don't want to hear your shit no more. I'm Steven Towndum, the guy who owns the city. He's gone to another place. Queer is where he represents."*

I asked him where he slept last night. *"In this piece of shit,"* he replied.

I asked him where he ate. *"I butt it with a piece of America. I wire food stamps from Bank of America. Some nigger doing her. I won't touch the dead branches of your filth."*

"THEN IN A MATTER OF 2001, ONE OF THESE LITTLE HELICOPTERS CAME DOWN AND SHOT ME IN THE BUTT WITH A BEANGUN." —ROBERT

"I have such an earnest world to live in. I have to look on. Eyes in the back of the head. Supposed to be productivity, but what is productivity? There's the idea that I need a brown eye and a debrowning.

"Have you ever been in a place and someone accosts you? I was wondering whether you had been repetitively set up by somebody who hits you. I did. I got six of them. Just recently out front here, someone came over and hit me aside the head. Just run over and hit me—repetitive the fellow jumped me violently out there—like a compliment, like a helicopter.

"I sleep beneath the overpass. But about three days ago it was during the daytime, you pass underneath the concrete was productive, and to pass out from underneath the concrete within just a matter of moments it was a feeling of lethargy. I had this dell system, a pack of little helicopters, put it through about a year ago. Three small ones and then like a round spinner machine, that's what it looked like. They have these like guns inside the two of them and about a dozen people originally picked me off. They fly up and they fly down. Then in a matter of 2001, one of these came down and shot me in the butt with a beangun and I declined going to anyone about it, at least machine going about it, because a machine shoots like that. But then within four months it shoots on the other side and maybe four months later they shoot in the shoulder and the fewpack waits around. Out of four of these available, it shot me in the middle of the back here, almost killed me. I laid over there and pretended to pass on, but there somehow muzzled off in the left side of the rear end. It's like a laser atrocity."

CONCLUSION

As the reader turns the last page of this book, I hope he or she thinks, "I suppose the people portrayed here are not so different from me. Maybe if I were as biologically vulnerable, if I had suffered one trauma after another as a child, if I were poor and didn't have a source of income or the means to get it, if I didn't have a family to stay with, I too might be living on the street. And if I lived on the street, I guess I'd look pretty dirty, and I might smell, and I'd probably be lugging around a cart, because where else would I keep my things? And if I slept on the street, exposed to the weather and the dirt and the grime, of course I'd get skin infections and look like I had some kind of pox. Of course my teeth would become abscessed and I'd have to get them pulled, particularly if I couldn't get Medicaid to fix them in a more sophisticated (and expensive) way. And of course I'd look weird and unapproachable. And if I didn't have any food and was hungry enough, I might dive into dumpsters for half-eaten sandwiches, grab meals at soup kitchens, steal, or panhandle.

"And perhaps if I had to face all this, day after day, and if I had suffered one loss after another, some admittedly by my own hand, I would be bored or miserable enough to dabble in drugs. And if this took the sting out of life, maybe I would do more than dabble. Maybe I'd get hooked. And if I did, I doubt I'd want to spend whatever handouts I was able to get on housing. Yeah, looked at in a certain way, I get all that."

If we could hear beyond the silence and see beyond the symptoms of the homeless mentally ill, we might be able to perceive the ways we are the same, not just the ways we are different. We'd be able to see that we all get cold when the temperature drops, wet and uncomfortable when it rains on us, and exhausted when we haven't slept. We'd be able to see that we all get hungry for food, affection, esteem, money—something. We'd have to acknowledge that we all have feelings, needs, and vulnerabilities; that we're all trying to make sense of our worlds; and that we all screw up and do things that make bad situations worse, take the wrong path, or fall off the horse and have trouble getting back on.

And if we understood all this, we might feel more connected to the people we now shun. We might identify with their predicaments. We might offer them more understanding and less blame. We might choose to include them in, rather than exclude them from, the spheres of life that are open to the rest of us. We might be more willing to share with them than withhold from them, and feel less resentful doing so.

And if our willingness to share extended to the political realm, we might make different decisions as a society. We might be more willing to enact legislation that would provide mentally ill people with decent housing, clothes, food, dental care, and mental health treatment. This, in turn, would make it easier for us to see what we have in common with them. Seeing them as fully human, we might also be less likely to segregate and punish them. We might conclude that they are entitled to a life of dignity, simply because they are human.

APPENDIX A

WHAT IS NEEDED

The gap between what we know can help people with serious mental illness and what we actually do to help them is enormous. While it is not the purpose of this book to offer a blueprint for what should be done, a few summary points are worth mentioning.

The bedrock of an effective community mental health system is case management. Never was a profession so perfectly misnamed, since the client is neither a "case" nor does he need to be "managed." The case manager fulfills crucial functions in the life of her client—as an advocate, a bridge between the client and services, a teacher, a friend, a guide, and a parental surrogate. There is nothing too big, too small, too dirty, or too mundane for her. What the client needs is what the case manager's role is.

It's a hard job, one for a smart, clinically trained, wise, well-balanced person who can empathize with those who often don't want empathy, can tolerate frustration and disappointment, is not afraid to get involved in the nitty-gritty of her clients' lives, and can commit her heart and brain to the work. In the first place, the case manager must engage clients who often want nothing to do with her and who have been taught through their experiences as children and as adults—and through the failures of the service system—not to trust anyone. They are certain they will eventually be deserted by anyone who offers help, and they have become experts at fulfilling this prophecy. Sometimes they don't get the help they need because they lack basic skills (like keeping track of time and showing up when and where they've agreed to do so); are driven by their anger to disappoint and thwart anyone who tries to help them; or are so overwhelmed by their psychiatric and drug-related symptoms that they simply can't cooperate, even with the most caring and sophisticated case manager. The case manager often has to scour the streets and the bars to find her clients, dealing with them *as* they are and *where* they are. This is the very nature of working with people who struggle with overwhelming impairments.

Assuming that, over time, the case manager is able to make some kind of human contact, perhaps through persistence, cajoling, or proving that she can help the client get SSI, housing, medication, or dental services, there is a chance that the client will begin to trust the case manager as a person. Without a real, human relationship, nothing else is possible. Only now can the case manager teach the person the skills that he either never developed or lost with the onset of his illness: how to shop, cook, do laundry, take care of an apartment, manage medications, budget money, take transportation, go to the movies, go to church or synagogue. And through this focus on concrete needs, the case manager helps the person develop skills relating to trust, attachment, social relationships, and resisting the craving for drugs. Finally, the case manager needs to help the person bridge the wide gap between his solitary life and inclusion in society, sometimes acting as a go-between, advocate, and negotiator to get him access to society's mainstream institutions and activities.

Without excellent case managers, a mental health system will tend to be mechanistic, inaccessible, and exclusively focused on the management of symptoms with medication, rather than also on clients' human development and rehabilitation. The core of clients' problems will be left untouched. The original promise of community mental health, inclusion, participation, and integration into society will be a distant memory. A service system deficient in many respects can be rescued by an excellent case management program. But if the latter is absent, there is little that the system can do to compensate.

It may seem obvious that homeless mentally ill people need a home, but housing has almost universally been one of the last services to be funded, perhaps because it is so expensive. And yet without housing, it is very difficult for people to remain clean and sober; to carry, store, and otherwise manage their medications; to keep their money safe; to take care of their physical health; to keep their teeth and gums healthy, etc. In addition to providing supportive housing, the government must set income support (e.g., SSI) at a reasonable level so that people are not driven into extreme poverty and kept there. The harsh conditions of poverty and the homelessness to which it often leads are so stressful that a high percentage of people will turn to street drugs in order to try to immunize themselves against these stresses.

Usually ignored when services are developed and funded, job training and supported employment (a system that helps people with disabilities achieve ongoing employment) are crucial parts of a service system. Work is so important to maintaining self-esteem, giving structure to a person's time, stabilizing symptoms, and supporting one's adaptive and executive functions, among many other things, that without it, people will be lacking a critical aspect of life. They will also be disregarded and demeaned by others, feel absolutely useless, and remain outsiders in a culture that promotes work. And yet getting businesses to provide supported employment opportunities, with some notable exceptions, has been almost impossible. Unless government actually incentivizes businesses to pitch in, with some form of tax credit, for example, it is unlikely that this gap will ever be filled.

Given the number of people with mental disorders in jails and prisons, the entire legal system as it relates to the mentally ill needs to be rethought: this includes the ways that criminal laws are enforced, the treatment that is provided to people in the correctional system, and the need for post-release planning and services. People with mental disorders are too frequently jailed for so-called nuisance crimes, ones without a victim that don't realistically justify jail sentences. Those who are jailed for reasonable cause should be treated during their incarcerations and then linked with services after their sentences have ended. The current practice of dumping people from jail onto the street with no money, no place to live, and no treatment almost ensures a revolving door in and out of jail.

The fight for basic services and subsistence has been so difficult that a fundamental rationale for deinstitutionalization has often been lost: for people with mental illness to be included in society. Living in society is very different from being included in society, the first being a geographic fact, the second a social one. Unless society is willing to actively involve people with mental illness in all spheres of social, political, and economic life, these individuals will continue to be deprived of one of their most important human rights. Participation in the workforce and inclusion in housing, neighborhoods, recreational activities, and religious institutions will require more than adequate mental health services. It will require something far more radical than a lack of discrimination against people with mental illness. Affirmative steps are required to pull people with serious mental illnesses back from the margins of society, where they currently exist. Actions must be taken to counter the constant social undertow that leads to their isolation, whether this occurs in mental hospitals, in jails, or on the street. Nor can these measures wait until people's symptoms are treated. Treatment cannot occur first and inclusion second. A broken leg will heal with or without social relationships, with or without inclusion in the community. A "broken mind" will not. Treatment for many people can only be accomplished in the context of inclusion. In order for this to occur, the community—not just the mentally ill individual—needs to change.

APPENDIX B

HISTORY OF THE HOMELESS MENTALLY ILL

The ebb and flow of contradictory and warring impulses toward people with mental disorders has been an enduring part of the American landscape for centuries: impulses to help and ignore, treat and mistreat, include and exclude, grant asylum and expose to harm. At different moments in our national history, one or the other of these forces has predominated. Even when prospects for fundamental reform appeared hopeful, even when public policy was primarily animated by therapeutic aspirations, the social stigma associated with mental disorders often acted as a drag on the actual implementation of these aims. The darker sentiments evoked by mental disorders that lay hidden, unacknowledged, and unexpressed within the social fabric would unexpectedly rise to the surface and hijack or vitiate the efforts at reform. The resulting compromise would bear only a dim resemblance to advocates' original intentions. Over time, as problems inherent in these half measures became visible, distasteful, or politically unpopular, a new and hopeful wave of reform would arise, only to be weakened by another undertow of resistance.

THE EMERGENCE OF THE ASYLUM: PROTECTION AND TREATMENT AT THE PRICE OF SOCIAL ISOLATION

The people represented in this book are, in part, the products of the aforementioned struggle between opposing social impulses. In America, these impulses can be traced back to the eighteenth and early nineteenth centuries. During that era, people with mental disorders who could not be cared for by their families or communities often ended up in almshouses or were imprisoned in jails. In these settings, they were frequently chained naked in cages, stalls, and pens; beaten with rods; lashed into obedience; and preyed upon by other residents.

Impassioned by these grim conditions, social activist Dorothea Dix, in the second quarter of the nineteenth century, successfully lobbied state legislatures to create asylums for the protection and treatment of people with mental disorders. At the outset, these public asylums were small, well-staffed hospitals that provided so-called "moral therapy," a kind of supportive, exhortative treatment based on the theory that mental disorders could be cured by caring staff in a stress-free environment. Many patients, after a relatively short period of hospitalization, were able to return to their families and communities in a considerably improved state.

Although the primary impetus behind the establishment of the asylums was benevolent, these facilities also served the less explicit but darker wish to isolate and segregate mentally ill people from the rest of society. Partially to satisfy these latter motivations and partially to achieve economic efficiencies, each hospital functioned like a walled medieval city, completely self-sufficient, with its own forest for lumber and firewood, its own farm animals and vegetable gardens for food, and its own laundry and kitchen. The success of this infrastructure depended on the unpaid labor of the more functional patients, who worked as lumberjacks, farmers, laundresses, maids, and cooks.

DETERIORATION OF THE ASYLUMS

After the Civil War, large waves of immigration, the economic recession of the 1870s, and other engines of social displacement combined to flood state hospitals with many more patients than they could handle. High admission rates in the face of limited staffing transformed these small, relatively humane asylums into large, understaffed, custodial, total institutions. In exchange for food, clothing, and shelter, patients became anonymous inmates with no civil rights, no autonomy, no privacy, little treatment, and no connections to their families and communities.

These conditions led to a vicious cycle of longer lengths of stay, larger patient populations, even less treatment, and in turn, even longer lengths of stay. Many patients who, in a previous era, would have been treated successfully and discharged became "incurable" and were transformed into lifelong residents under these adverse conditions. The sense of therapeutic pessimism engendered by this situation became a self-fulfilling prophecy. State governments seized upon it as an excuse to justify their unwillingness to provide adequate funding.

Originally created as small therapeutic asylums, by the early 1900s, these institutions became large dumping grounds used by states for the social exclusion, social control, and social welfare of a broad swath of the population who were suffering from mental disorders, alcoholism, mental retardation, epilepsy, and neurosyphilis and other forms of dementia. They also housed many individuals who were simply elderly and infirm, who lacked a source of social or economic support, or who were unacceptably deviant for one reason or another. By the mid-twentieth century, the unacknowledged impulses that had contributed to the creation of state hospitals in the first place became their predominant function. Social rejects, including the mentally ill, were segregated from society, often for their entire lives.

Given the deterioration in the conditions and reputation of state hospitals, it was probably inevitable that coercion would become their primary means of patient admission. Commitment generally took place without explicit standards and through no formal legal procedure. Moreover, there was no independent judicial review of patients' continuing commitment. Once they were locked inside the hospital, it was often very difficult to get out.

In summary, within a hundred years, almost every characteristic of state hospitals was transformed: their size, staffing, treatment, culture, and legal authority; the length of patient stay; the characteristics of their residents; and the functions that society expected of them.

DEINSTITUTIONALIZATION: EARLY ROOTS

By 1955, the population of state hospitals had climbed to 560,000. At this time, it was serendipitously discovered that the anesthetic chlorpromazine (Thorazine) could ameliorate the psychotic symptoms of certain patients, even some who had been considered completely hopeless. For the first time, more patients were discharged from than admitted to state hospitals. The process of deinstitutionalization had begun.

Consisting of the large-scale discharge of patients from state hospitals and a restriction in the number of new admissions, the policy and process of deinstitutionalization quickly steamrolled across the country. One of the important reasons for its widespread adoption was its broad appeal to parts of society that were generally on opposite sides of the political spectrum. State governments supported deinstitutionalization as a way of reining in the growing costs of public hospitalization. Civil rights attorneys seized upon it as a way of eliminating an abusive deprivation of liberty. Mental health professionals promoted it as a way of freeing up money from a failed institutional system to fund a modern community treatment system.

The political alliance among these groups ultimately came apart when it became clear that the savings anticipated from reduced state hospital populations were not materializing. The fixed costs of these facilities remained high and couldn't be redirected to create community services. Faced with this fiscal reality, state governments argued that it was no longer their responsibility to take care of patients once they had been discharged. This stance was viewed by mental health professionals, patients, and patients' families as a deep betrayal. Their support for deinstitutionalization had in part been predicated on the promise that funding would follow patients out of the hospital into the community. While the more functional patients flourished simply being freed from an adverse environment, many less functional patients suffered. They found themselves as isolated in their new communities as they had been in their old state hospitals. As a result of aggressive discharge and restrictive admission policies, the state hospital population in the United States declined from 560,000 in 1960 to 53,000 in 1993. Before long, without services, the number of casualties in cities and towns began to mount.

THE DRUG EPIDEMIC

Community life was bound to be difficult for people who had spent years segregated from it, but the drug epidemic that developed in the 1970s and that continues to this day made things infinitely worse. It transformed the face of mental disorders and altered the course of deinstitutionalization in the United States. Before long, almost 70 percent of people hospitalized for serious mental disorders also had a diagnosis of substance abuse disorder. A high proportion of patients found the side effects of psychiatric medications intolerable and were constantly reminded by these medications that they were "crazy" and would be so until the day they died. Many turned to street drugs as a physically and emotionally comforting (and culturally acceptable) way to alter their states of consciousness.

While affording temporary subjective relief to many people, street drugs rendered the intrinsically complex problems of mental disorders even more difficult to treat. These drugs frequently aggravated underlying psychiatric symptoms, further compromised patients' diminished sense of reality and impulse control, and weakened their motivation for treatment. They also increased patients' vulnerability to predators on the street, involved them in criminal activities, pushed them into the arms of the correctional system, and increased their risk of dying from drug-related complications. Drugs, mental disorders, homelessness, and incarceration became a vicious cycle from which many never escaped.

THE FEDERAL RESPONSE: TOO LITTLE, TOO LATE

As long as patients were living in mental hospitals operated by state governments, the problems of the mentally ill were historically defined as a state responsibility. But once these patients were discharged into communities, states tried to divest themselves of responsibility for them. Responding to the political pressure generated by the large number of poor, untreated patients in the community, the federal government, for the first time, began to accept some responsibility for their welfare. Over the past 60 years, Congress has enacted legislation to ameliorate some of the harshest conditions: the federal Community Mental Health Centers Act, the Medicaid and Medicare acts, the Supplemental Security Income Act, and low-income housing appropriations. This legislation was groundbreaking and helped to address the many life problems of disabled people in the community, but the stigma of mental disorders and society's resulting ambivalence toward people suffering from them were such that these efforts never went far enough. Adequate treatment, housing, jobs, and economic support largely remained unrealized ideals. Hundreds of thousands of untreated mentally ill people were forced by their poverty to live in dilapidated transient hotels with no private bathrooms, showers, or kitchens. Worse, they drifted to the street, where they lived with nothing.

SHELTERS: BETTER THAN THE STREET?

To save people from the cruelest conditions of the street, many cities created temporary shelters. Unfortunately, these settings were often poorly designed, poorly funded, and frequently harsh in other ways. They often excluded people who were actively using drugs. They were closed to other people because they didn't have enough beds. Sleeping spaces were assigned on a first come, first serve basis to people who had to stand in line for several hours, often outdoors, before they learned whether there was a bed available for them that night. People who didn't make the cut were turned away. Those who did were only marginally more fortunate, for they were often stuffed into beds so close together that these individuals were in perpetual danger of contracting each other's contagious diseases. People with certain kinds of mental disorders who were particularly frightened of getting too close to other people, physically or emotionally, couldn't tolerate such intimate sleeping arrangements. Many shelters developed the reputation of being poorly supervised and, frankly, dangerous. They often failed to provide locked personal storage space, making everyone's possessions vulnerable to theft. Many people refused to use shelters after repeated experiences of "losing" what few possessions they had. One of the most aggravating but common practices of shelters was to turn out their "guests" early in the morning, no matter how inclement the weather. In the afternoon, the process of lining up would begin again. For all of these reasons, the shelter system was, and too often continues to be, an unreliable, dangerous, punishing, and humiliating experience. Over the years, thousands of people simply gave up on them and decided to take their chances outside, even though sleeping on the street was a grueling, physically demanding, emotionally stressful, demeaning, and dangerous existence.

THE EMERGENCE OF GENERAL MEDICAL HOSPITALS FOR ACUTE PSYCHIATRIC PATIENTS

During the same time frame that shelters and other parts of the social service system were struggling for funding, the health care system was gaining an increasing share of society's resources. Private and public hospital reimbursement became available for psychiatric patients. At the same time, general medical hospitals were facing a declining length of stay for medical and surgical patients. This led to an increase in the number of empty beds, a trend that presented these hospitals with a need for a new cohort of patients. Psychiatric patients, whose treatment was increasingly being reimbursed by the private and public sectors, were obvious candidates to fill this niche and quickly became its beneficiaries. Within 60 years, general hospitals converted many of their empty medical/surgical beds into psychiatric beds within small, 20-patient units. By 1998, the number of psychiatric beds within general hospitals grew from just about zero to 54,434. Inpatient beds in private psychiatric hospitals also increased, from 14,295 in 1970 to a high of 45,000 in 1990, before dropping back down to 25,095 in 2002. Most patients who needed hospitalization and who previously had been admitted to large public institutions were admitted instead to general hospital psychiatric units and to private psychiatric hospitals.

While in no way offsetting the dramatic decrease in state hospital beds, the use of general hospitals for psychiatric patients represented a real improvement for those who could gain admission. Many patients needing psychiatric treatment could be cared for in their local communities, where families could visit them, and from which it was logistically easier to plan for aftercare services. The integration of psychiatric patients into general community medical hospitals reduced some of the stigma associated with mental disorders by "medicalizing" their image, and also brought inpatient psychiatric care into the mainstream of modern medicine. Psychiatric units in general hospitals were required by hospital accrediting organizations to meet the more exacting staffing and treatment standards that had for a long time exclusively protected physically ill patients. This made it easier to attract high-quality medical, nursing, and social work staff than it had been in state hospitals.

Over time, private and public funding organizations became less willing to pay for the psychiatric inpatient treatment that had made possible this increased quality of care. As a result, general hospitals decreased the length of time psychiatric patients could be hospitalized—from an average of 30 days to an average of 5 days. Large numbers of patients were admitted and discharged so rapidly that it was impossible for many of them to be stabilized before being sent back to their homes, shelters, or the street. A 30-percent readmission rate within one month after discharge became a common phenomenon for psychiatric patients in urban general hospitals.

THE TILT TOWARD CIVIL LIBERTIES AND ITS UNINTENDED CONSEQUENCES

Another phenomenon that contributed to the growing number of untreated patients in the community was the enactment of more rigorous civil commitment laws. These laws made it more difficult to commit patients to hospitals and restricted the time they could be confined there even if funding was available to pay for it. Physicians were required to substantiate with hard, behavioral evidence mentally ill people's imminent threat of serious physical harm to themselves or others, or their inability to meet their basic needs for food, safety, and shelter. Unless people met these rigorous standards, they could not be hospitalized against their will no matter how psychotic they were.

This increased respect for civil rights prevented unnecessary hospitalizations, but often at the expense of people's mental health. Were adequate alternatives available, it would have been possible to treat many mentally ill people on a voluntary outpatient basis without either restricting their liberty through forced hospitalization or abandoning them because they failed to meet standards for commitment. The choice of involuntary hospitalization or no treatment at all, which prevailed during most of the state-hospital era, is being repeated today in the general-hospital era.

CRIMINALIZATION OF THE MENTALLY ILL: FULL TURN OF THE WHEEL OF HISTORY

In the end, many people were not spared a restriction of their liberty, even when they couldn't be hospitalized against their will. Tighter commitment standards, designed to decrease involuntary confinement in hospitals, ironically led to increased involuntary confinement in jails and prisons. The police in many cities, learning that hospitals could no longer commit certain patients, brought them to jail instead. Sleeping in public places, shoplifting, urinating on the street, or just acting crazy was often enough to trigger the arrest of a person with a mental disorder. People gained their freedom from one institution only to lose it to another.

Back-door violations of patients' civil rights were not the only consequence of the shift from hospitals to jails. The mental disorders that led to arrest in the first place were often aggravated by the crowded and punitive conditions of many correctional institutions. People with mental disorders often became the butt of abuse by other inmates. Moreover, because psychiatric services in most jails were, and continue to be, minimal, people with mental disorders frequently remained highly symptomatic and were forced to endure prolonged suffering as a result. Incarceration also entailed a loss of their Medicaid and SSI benefits, requiring that they begin the lengthy and complicated process of reinstatement of these benefits all over again at the end of their sentences. Some people had the ability to do this; others didn't and were, consequently, poorer and more vulnerable in every respect at the end of their incarceration than before it. Finally, jails had very limited capacity to help them prepare for community life after their release. People were typically dumped out of their cells at the end of their jail or prison terms with $50 in their pockets, a single change of clothes, no place to go, no health or welfare benefits, and no link with mental health treatment other than an address or telephone number of some agency. The entire process was a setup for further deterioration, violations of the law, and then reincarceration.

The numbers of mentally ill people in the criminal justice system today are staggering. Some jails now house more mentally ill people than any state or private psychiatric hospital in the country. Between 10 and 16 percent of inmates have mental disorders. Forty percent of white women aged 24 and younger in state prisons are mentally ill. In 1998, while fewer than 55,000 people were receiving treatment in psychiatric hospitals at any given time, 283,000 mentally ill people, almost five times that number, were serving time in jails and prisons, and an additional 547,000 were on probation. The wheel of history that began revolving in the eighteenth and early nineteenth centuries with mentally ill people in jails had turned a full revolution by the 1980s. Mentally ill people were back in jail in even larger numbers.

It is generally agreed that the use of jails for most people who are mentally ill is ineffective as a deterrent, counterproductive as an economic policy, harmful as a clinical intervention, and offensive to the most elementary sense of justice. Nevertheless, this form of isolating and confining people with mental disorders continues to operate largely under the radar, without much public outcry. Perhaps jail is where the public feels they really belong. Perhaps their confinement reassures us they cannot hurt us. Perhaps when they're in jail, we don't have to see them.

THE CYCLE OF HOMELESSNESS

Approximately 200,000 of the estimated 750,000 to 2,000,000 homeless people in the United States at any given time are severely mentally ill, and an even larger number have complex substance abuse disorders. The appearance of homelessness in American cities began in the 1970s and resulted from the interaction of many factors that produced large numbers of very poor, untreated, drug-addicted, mentally ill people who had no place to go but the street. Among these factors were the following:

1. The policy of deinstitutionalization adopted by state governments, which led to the discharge of hundreds of thousands of patients from state mental hospitals and made it difficult for patients to gain admission or readmission to these facilities—and the absence of community services available to these people, specifically the dearth of case management

2. The difficulty experienced by families in caring for their mentally ill relatives, whose constant crises and complicated symptoms often led to ruptured relationships and lost financial and emotional support

3. The reluctance of many mentally ill people to take psychiatric medications, in part because of the drugs' disturbing side effects

4. The epidemic of street drugs, leading to dependence on or addiction to these substances, which provided some temporary relief but tended over time to aggravate peoples' psychiatric symptoms and pull them into life on the street

5. The enactment of stringent commitment laws that made it difficult for hospitals to admit very symptomatic people against their will unless they were a clear and immediate danger to themselves or others

6. Discrimination against mentally ill patients by insurance companies, and by state and federal governments through Medicare and Medicaid policies, making it financially disadvantageous for general hospitals to admit many very needy patients

7. The pressure placed on general hospitals by these same entities to discharge patients prematurely, often after just a few days, even before medications had had time to relieve their symptoms and before hospital staff were able to carefully plan for their aftercare—phenomena that often led to their being returned to the street and the stressful, drug-addicted life that was often the reason they needed psychiatric hospitalization in the first place

8. The lack of administrative mechanisms to assure "continuity of care" between hospitals and outpatient services, leading to a situation in which many patients fell through the cracks and ended up on the street

9. A system of traditional outpatient clinics with staff administratively bound to their desks, unable to provide outreach and help mentally ill patients gain access

to SSI, housing, drug treatment, job training, and other services necessary for day-to-day functioning

10. The dearth of low-income housing due to gentrification of the urban housing stock and the failure of government to provide sufficient subsidized housing

11. The constant underfunding of SSI, the federal and state welfare program upon which most severely mentally ill people depended and that forced them to choose between housing and other needs

12. The increasing tendency of society to criminalize the mentally ill (i.e., to lock them up for minor crimes) and then dump them back into the street at the end of their sentences with no money, no treatment, and no housing

13. The development of a so-called shelter system, which many mentally ill people found dangerous and thus unacceptable as an alternative to the street

In summary, homelessness was the result of the way broad social and economic factors interacted with a succession of incomplete reforms in which people were moved from poor-houses in the eighteenth century to overcrowded asylums in the nineteenth century, to shelters, prisons, and the street in the latter half of the twentieth century. Ironically, while homelessness evokes public sympathy as an abstract matter, homeless individuals seem to elicit revulsion when we see them in the flesh. The social stigma that underlies this reaction, and its political and economic consequences for the mentally ill, have been major culprits in this tragic drama. Clearly, the current situation is not simply a result of one mistake or misguided public policy: it is the combined effect of many factors involving the prejudices of the culture, and the policies and budgets of multiple governmental systems (health care, mental health, social welfare, employment, public housing, public works, criminal justice, and correctional). The casualties we see on the street reflect a social consensus that the current conditions of mentally ill people in America are tolerable, and that these people don't deserve more than they're getting.

The drastic effects of homelessness on every aspect of the lives of the mentally ill cannot be overstated. In addition to compromising their physical health and fragile psychological stability, living on the street increased their illegal drug use and made it difficult for them to keep appointments, access services, and find and maintain employment. Homelessness also made it impossible for those people who were willing to take psychiatric medications to store, carry, and take them. Medications were often lost, stolen, traded for illegal drugs, or simply forgotten in the chaos of street life.

These and other consequences of homelessness made it difficult for mentally ill people to "pull themselves together" and escape their grim living situations. Life on the street became a self-perpetuating condition. The longer people spent on the street, the harder it was to get off. The end of this cycle was often not just hospitalization or jail, but death. The mortality rate among homeless mentally ill people has been estimated at 3.5 times that of the general population in one city where it was intensively studied.

ACKNOWLEDGMENTS

Thank you to Dorothy Dundas, whose life story exemplifies courage and compassion, and whose wise consultation and encouragement were vital throughout this project.

To my dear friend Elizabeth Marcus, whose criticism was unsparing and honest. This expression of her friendship contributed greatly to the overall conception of the book.

To my companion and colleague Dr. Stephen Green, who generously consulted with me with the eye of both a photographer and a psychiatrist.

To my joyful, smart, and loving friend Elena Portacolone, who read my manuscript word for word and gave me invaluable advice on how to improve it.

To my photography mentor, Donald Kennedy, who accompanied me on the street in the early days of the project and taught me everything I came to know about photography.

To my dear companion Steve Bearman, who provided me with the friendship, support, and insight I needed to face down my demons in writing this book.

To my colleagues Alicia Boccellari, Kathy O'Brien, and the San Francisco General Hospital Emergency Department Case Management staff, whose tenacious, wise, and sensitive clinical work saved the lives of several people featured in this book.

To my daughter, Laura, and my son, Justin, and his wife, Laurie, who reviewed draft after draft, provided me with crucial feedback, and never gave up on my vision for this project.

To my sister, Nicki, my brother-in-law, Gerard, my brother, Ken, and my sister-in-law, Elaine, who have supported and encouraged me over the years, who lifted my spirits when they had plummeted, and who always believed that this book had something of importance to say.

And to my mother and father, whose values, courage, and willingness to stand up for what they believed set me on a path for life.

ABOUT THE AUTHOR

Robert L. Okin, MD, was born in the Bronx, New York. He attended college and medical school at the University of Chicago, and after a psychiatric residency at the Albert Einstein College of Medicine in New York City, he spent two years at the National Institute of Mental Health, where he became interested in community psychiatry.

Early in his career, Dr. Okin was appointed commissioner of mental health for Vermont, and then for Massachusetts, where he led the development of community-based services for people who had previously spent years in public mental hospitals. He was one of the first commissioners to recognize the need for supportive housing for these people and to advocate for its creation.

A leading psychiatrist and internationally known expert on mental health service reform, Dr. Okin is a founding member of the board of advisors of Mental Disability Rights International (MDRI). He served as MDRI's lead psychiatric expert on technical assistance projects and investigative missions in Armenia, Azerbaijan, Hungary, Mexico, Paraguay, Peru, Romania, Turkey, and Ukraine.

Following the release of MDRI's report on Mexico in 2000, Dr. Okin served as an expert consultant to the Mexican government and helped close the abusive Ocaranza psychiatric facility in the state of Hidalgo, replacing it with more homelike settings and community-based services. In Paraguay, Dr. Okin helped MDRI negotiate a historic settlement agreement through the Inter-American Commission on Human Rights. As part of the settlement in 2005, Paraguay agreed to a number of improvements in its treatment of the mentally ill, including restructuring the national mental health service system, creating community services, and downsizing the country's main psychiatric facility.

Dr. Okin was chief of service of the San Francisco General Hospital Department of Psychiatry; professor of clinical psychiatry at the University of California, San Francisco; and vice chair of the University of California, San Francisco, School of Medicine's Department of Psychiatry, where he oversaw the development of crucial services for San Francisco's most acutely and chronically mentally ill patients, including the SFGH Department of Psychiatry's Emergency Department Case Management Program (which received the National Association of Public Hospitals and Health Systems' Safety Net Award in 1999).

As a world-recognized expert on human rights for the mentally disabled, Dr. Okin helped develop an international consensus statement condemning the use of electroconvulsive therapy without anesthesia. He has been quoted numerous times in the *New York Times*, was featured on ABC's *20/20* about his efforts to close down Ocaranza and help former residents live in the community, and has published numerous papers in psychiatric journals. In 2009, he received the American Psychiatric Association's prestigious Human Rights Award.

Dr. Okin lives in Northern California and has two grown children, Laura and Justin, and a young stepson, Oliver.